Highland Man

Richard 1987

Contents

Highland Life Series

Highland Man
by Ian Grimble

Published by the
Highlands and Islands Development
Board
Bridge House, Bank Street, Inverness

First published 1980
© 1980 Ian Grimble

Also in the Highland Life Series
Highland Birds
Highland Animals
Highland Landforms
Highland Flora

Designed by
Mackay Design Associates Ltd

Printed by Morrison & Gibb Ltd
Edinburgh and London

ISBN 0 902347 66 7

Preface

From a publication of 1822: 'For seven centuries Birnam Hill, at the entrance into Athol, has formed the boundary between the Lowlands and the Highlands, and between the Saxon and Gaelic languages. On the south and east sides of the hill, breeches are worn and the Scottish Lowland dialect spoken with as broad an accent as in Mid-Lothian. On the north and west sides are found the Gaelic, the kilt and the plaid, with all the peculiarities of the Highland character.'*

Exaggerations there certainly are in this contrast, more so now than when it was written. Nevertheless it contains a core of truth. Highland Man deals, in the main, with the early influences which explain the contrasts and the conformities embodied in Scottishness, and in particular with what is distinctively Highland in our historical origins and development.

Ian Grimble has combined scholarship and literary skill in laying out the roots of settlement and civilisation in the Highlands and Islands. The illustrations are aposite and effective reinforcements of the text. Within the broad historical sweep of the text room is found for fascinating asides, for example on close similarities between Hindu and Gaelic law. The reader is left with a profound respect for the early forebears, Celtic, Pictish, Scottish and Norse, of today's Highlander and Islander.

As the author says in rounding-off their story these inheritors 'have preserved to this day a distinct identity and an indomitable pride in their heritage despite the battering they were to receive during the next six centuries of history.' Highland Man adds its own valuable contribution to that identity and heritage by telling its story in such a clear and compelling way. The Highlands and Islands Development Board takes pride in having initiated this series and this final volume.

Kenneth Alexander.

*D Stewart, Sketches of the Character, Manners and Present State of the Highlanders of Scotland. Edinburgh, Archibald Constable and Co., 1822, 2 vol.

Foreword

The author Dr Ian Grimble was born in Hong Kong of colonial Scottish ancestry. He took his degree in History at Balliol College, Oxford, and was awarded his PH.D. at Aberdeen University for his thesis on *Gaelic Society in the Northern Highlands*. Later, he was to expand his research material in *The Trial of Patrick Sellar*, 1962, in *Chief of Mackay*, 1965, and in *The World of Rob Donn*, 1979. In 1967 he co-edited *The Future of the Highlands* with Professor D S Thomson. *Scottish Clans and Tartans* was published in 1973.

In the field of television Dr Grimble has contributed many series of historical programmes notably *Who are the Scots?*, which was first transmitted in 1971 and repeated in 1976; *The Scottish Nation* in 1972; *Kings, Lords and Commoners* in 1971-2; *Grimble on Genius* in 1979. In radio, his series on *Regency People* was published by the B.B.C. in 1972.

Dr Grimble made his home for twenty years in the Mackay country of northern Sutherland and has been made Honorary Member of the Clan Mackay Society. He is also a Fellow of the Royal Historical Society and was elected President of the Edinburgh Sir Walter Scott Club for 1976-7.

As a social historian with an obvious deep love of the Highlands and Islands he has presented a broad social history of the Region in popular lectures and illustrated talks and through publications and recordings prepared specially for the Highlands and Islands Development Board—*Highland History*, a touring map which illustrates ancient artifacts and interesting archaeological and historical sites and includes a history of the Region from early times to 1745; and recordings in the Highland Man series, available in cassette form. In one of these he travels through the Great Glen tracing the history of the 1715 and 1745 rebellions. In the other he presents the folk music of the region.

In this essay, his latest work to be published by the Highlands and Islands Development Board, Dr Grimble tells the story of man in the Region from the time of the earliest known people to A.D. 1300 and the end of autonomous rule.

The first people who can be said with certainty to have lived in the Highlands and Islands are small kinship groups of Mesolithic nomads, hunters, fishers and food gatherers. Some of them stayed for a time in the Oban area and on the nearby islands, leaving traces of their brief occupation in refuse shell heaps, flint scatters, flint tools and antler fish spears. The first men to leave substantial evidence of a settled existence are the Neolithic farmers who appeared about 4000 B.C. and soon afterwards began to build the varied and numerous chambered tombs, an architectural form seen today at its most spectacular at Maes Howe on Orkney.

The arrival of the Beaker people with their distinctive pottery and metal tools heralded the start of the Bronze Age in all but the most northerly stone-using communities. The newcomers, though practising a different religion, often made use of the tombs of the earlier settlers. Some of their pottery has been also found in those other imposing monuments to Late Neolithic and Early Bronze Age man, the stone circles for which there is evidence of an astronomical use that was to decline with the onset of a climatic deterioration around 1500 B.C.

A second, more serious deterioration in the 7th Century B.C. affected most of Europe and resulted eventually in the arrival of Celtic speaking newcomers, the introduction of iron and the development of fortifications which were to culminate in the magnificent, impregnable brochs that are peculiar to Scotland and almost all of which are found in the Highlands and Islands.

Agricula's victory over Calgacus at Mons Graupius (sometimes identified as Duncrub Hill, Perthshire) was never consolidated and so whilst southern Britain fell completely under Roman influence it was felt only indirectly in the Highlands and Islands. Without its constraints, both here and in unconquered Ireland, Celtic art flourished to reach a new peak with the advent of Christianity.

The period of the Viking invasion and the settlement of large areas of the Highlands and Islands forms the penultimate chapter of Dr Grimble's story. Its effects, however, continue to be felt through to the closing paragraphs, the death of Margaret, the Little Maid of Norway and queen to be, and the what-might-have-been question if this daughter of the King of Norway had lived to reign as Queen of Scots.

First Footers

Today we can travel from one end of the British Isles to the other in a few hours; yet people were living in the south of England almost five hundred thousand years before the first men we know of ventured into the Highlands and Islands. The explanation for this astonishing time-lag most probably lies in the succession of ice ages that sealed the north of the British Isles at a time when they were still joined to the continent of Europe. As the glaciers retreated towards their present position, the sea gradually encroached on the North Sea plain, which had stretched from England across to Scandinavia, and, finally, in about 5000 B.C. and several thousand years after the gradual process had begun, it broke through our remaining land link with the continent to form the English Channel.

Beyond ice-sheets that had extended at one time over all but the most southerly parts of Britain, people had inhabited an arctic landscape resembling the Russian tundra. Imperceptibly the weather grew warmer and forests of birch and pine spread over the land as far as Shetland though, in the north, the forest was replaced by moorland before man's arrival, while in the south of Scotland the pine gave way to alder. The reindeer, man's prey in the tundra, barely outlived the ice ages. It survived longest in the most northern and open parts of the Highlands but there, too, it would eventually die out. Man was forced to change to hunting forest animals, slowly and somewhat belatedly, wandering further and further north in search of the wild boar, wild oxen and deer which were already well established in the younger forest areas.

It is not possible, of course, precisely to plot the routes, coastal or inland, taken by any single group in their movements about the Highlands. We do know, however, that it was not until about 6500 B.C. that a group or groups of them reached Oban and the islands beyond. It is from this time that our record of them begins. This does not mean that these people were necessarily the very first ever to set foot in the Highlands and Islands but simply that they left in their refuse heaps along the coast some of the earliest evidence of a human presence yet discovered. We call these early inhabitants 'mesolithic' because they lived out their short nomadic existence in the middle period between the paeolithic peoples of an earlier age in which, as far as we know, Scotland was uninhabited, and the later neolithic folk of the final era of stone-using man. Nothing has been found so far to indicate that they brought with them the artistic skills of palaeolithic man on the continent, the wonderful gift for portraying animals that can still be seen on the walls of caves in France and Spain, but they were by no means unaccomplished. Indeed it is from their traditional skills in making tools and weapons that we can discern links with differing though overlapping cultural backgrounds and with continental locations as widely spaced as northern Spain and the Baltic. At Campbeltown in Kintyre they made stout flint tools very much like those of the roughly contemporary people of Northern Ireland. In the area of Oban they fashioned antler and bone into barbed heads for their fish-spears in the manner of a much earlier people who lived in what is now the Basque country of the Franco-Spanish border. Finds elsewhere in Scotland show that they were familiar with a form of axe, made from the antlers of the red deer, which appears to originate with a forest dwelling people of Scandinavia and the Baltic.

Gradually, from scant evidence, a picture of our few mesolithic dispersed Highlanders and Islanders begins to emerge and if it shows them merely to be a mixed bag made up of small, scattered bands of food scavengers this is a gross over-simplification. It is all too easy for modern man to underestimate them. Someone not long ago described their lives as 'solitary, poor, nasty, brutish and short'. It is true that their lives were short; their average life expectancy was probably not much more than twenty-five years and few could have lived much beyond their thirtieth year. Equally so, one might agree that their lives were solitary since there was probably not more than fifty to a hundred of them dispersed about the Highlands in small 'family' groups of twenty or so, but 'solitary', 'poor', 'nasty' are all relative, if not quite irrelevant, terms to apply to these people. They were nomads who, more or less constantly involved in a ceaseless

Europe under ice

Britain remained joined to the continent with the R. Thames a tributary of the Rhine, long after the southern ice had begun to retreat some twenty thousand years ago. About six thousand years later, mammoth appeared in the Scottish tundra and, despite yielding twice in the next few thousand years to re-advancing ice, the renewal of life was speeded by the climate, by the propagating frame of the South which had not lain under ice, by the land bridges that existed at the time and by the mineral-rich soil ground from the rocks by the glaciers.

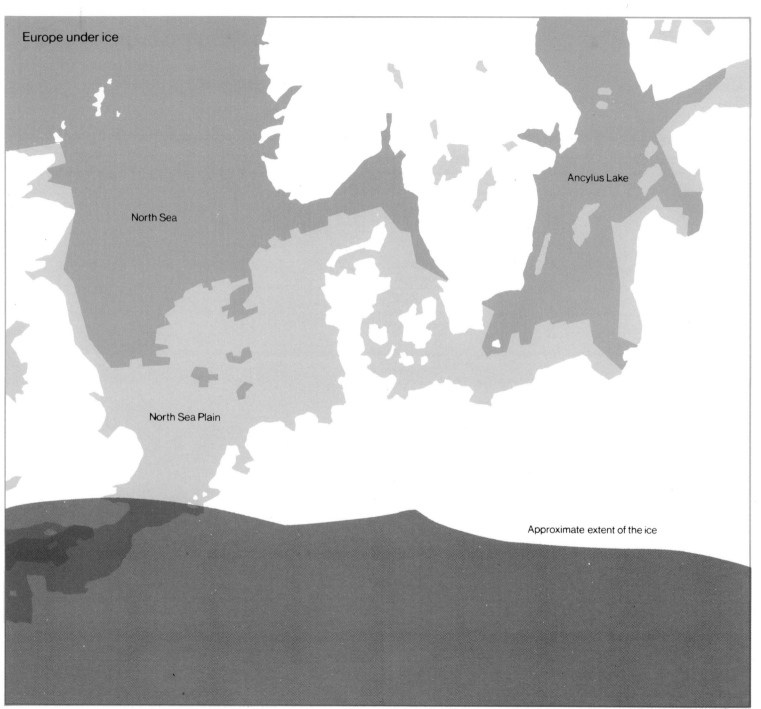

Europe under ice

North Sea

Ancylus Lake

North Sea Plain

Approximate extent of the ice

Mesolithic implements found at Risga, Oronsay and Oban: a fish-hook and two bone tools; a stone hand-hammer, antler mattock and pieces of a barbed antler harpoon with holes for a line in the butt.

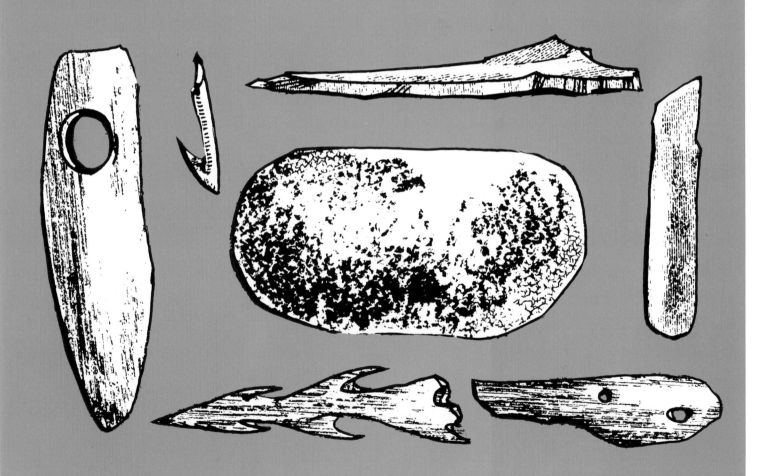

Traces of mesolithic man's presence near Oban and on Colonsay, Oronsay, Islay, Tiree, Coll, Skye and Lewis show his apparent preference for island sites and for open shores many of which we see as raised beaches seven to fifteen metres higher than they were in his day. But our coastline has undergone many changes; the rise in the land released from the enormous weight of ice is partly obscured by the great rise in the post-glacial sea level. Ten thousand years before mesolithic man hunted the island shores the level of the sea was 50 m lower; Skye and Mull would have been peninsulas and a land bridge most probably joined Argyll and Ireland.

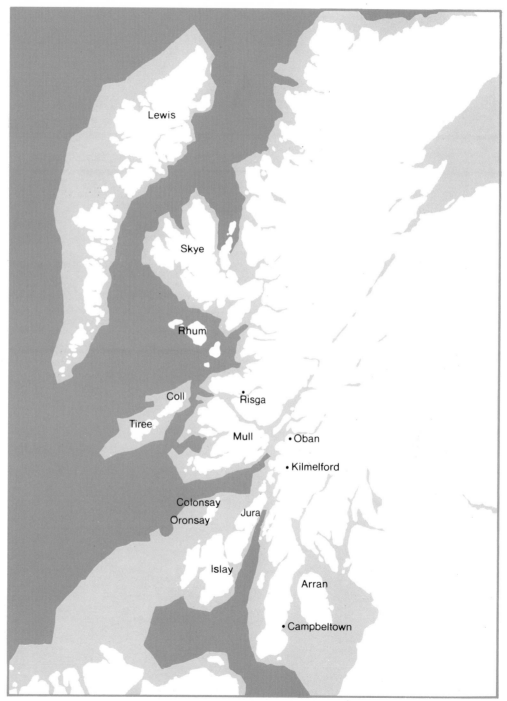

search for food, had not reached the stage at which they might settle to farm crops and breed cattle. They were nonetheless *Homo sapiens sapiens*, skilled and reasoning beings. They attacked, for example, their open forest environment with antler axes and fire not out of mindless violence but for a very good reason. It temporarily cleared the land and stimulated new growth, which, in turn, encouraged the wild-life and so made for better hunting. If they lived in caves around Oban it was because the caves were there. Where there were no such natural shelters, as on Oronsay, they built their own. They were, in fact, creatures of resourceful intelligence.

Apart from hunting game of the forests, they trapped birds and, with bone and antler tackle, caught a variety of fish from canoes hollowed from the trunks of trees. Several dugout canoes have been found in the Firth of Clyde and these, although of a later period, help us towards a clearer understanding of just how little earlier men could have taken with them as they moved from one place to another and also of the hazards which would inevitably

have to be faced on fishing expeditions or, possibly, as they sought the precious pitch-stone of Arran and the bloodstone of Rhum. No doubt it took courage and a kind of sea-manship to navigate these craft. It also took no small skill and much patient labour to shape and hollow out their canoes even with the controlled assistance of fire.

Archaeologists have suggested that they could also have made boats by stretching hides or skins over wooden frames in a way similar to the technique of making the curragh, or coracle, which may still be seen in use today in parts of Ireland. Unfortunately our record of their lives is meagre and no examples of such skin boats from this period have yet come to light. The same is true, too, of their dug-outs, but here we are on firmer ground. We know that these people had the skill, the tools and the material with which to make canoes. We know also that they must have had boats of some kind since small groups of them crossed to Jura and the smaller island of Oronsay and, during their stay, ate fish which can only be caught by deep water angling. Bones from their refuse heaps show that their diet included sea bream, salmon, haddock, wrasse, conger, ray, skate and sharks. Perhaps the black sea bream could have been caught from the rocks around the coast and so could some of the edible deep water crab they occasionally enjoyed, but not many of the others.

A providential addition to the larder of meso-lithic man, not only in the Highlands but in Scotland as a whole and in Scandinavia, came with the finding of a stranded whale. Just outside our area, along twelve miles of the Firth of Forth, there was a notorious, natural death-trap for these large but comparatively docile creatures where there were frequent strandings. Although they were possibly rather less frequent on the beaches of the Highlands and Islands, they were nonetheless welcome and exciting events. The carcass stripped with antler axes meant a temporary relaxing of a group's food gathering activities, but such bonuses were not everyday occur-rences. Mesolithic man was more often called upon to act directly and positively relying more on seal hunts for the rich meat and

A form of prehistoric dug-out canoe.

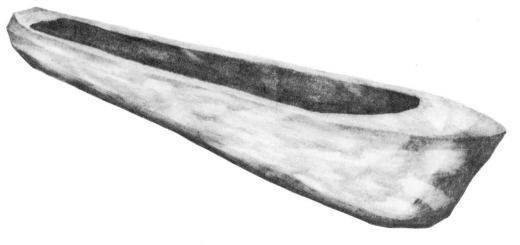

10

The dug-out canoe, a form of which is shown on the previous page, and the coracle, illustrated here in the modern Welsh form, were two of man's earliest craft. Those who know the often dangerous waters around the camp sites of mesolithic man in the Highlands and Islands suggest that he would have found the coracle, a framework of withies covered with hide, not only easier to handle on land but a great deal safer to navigate than the narrow-beam dug-out.

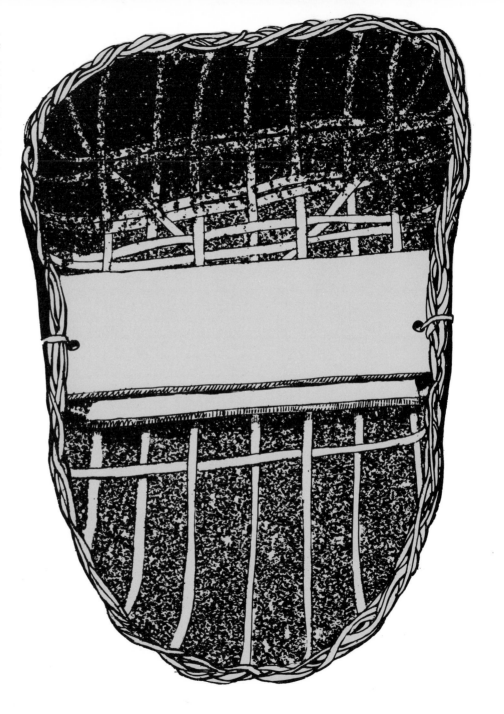

Now extinct, the Great Auk would have been easy prey to prehistoric hunters in northern Atlantic areas; a flightless diving bird, its movements out of the water were slow and awkward.

blubber than on providence; or, perhaps, on catching the now extinct Great Auk, a flightless diving bird which, because of its slow and clumsy movements out of the water, became easy prey during its mating season on land. These rich pickings, however, form only a small part of the diet of those Obanians we know of. To judge from their large refuse shell-heaps, shellfish were a most important food to them. At first sight the shell-heaps may seem disproportionately large. After all the groups that left them were small and their stay was not particularly long. On the other hand, it would take about seventy limpets, laboriously prised from the rocks, to make the equivalent of half a pound of meat.

Another form of refuse that a few people could collect in large quantities was the chippings of toolmakers. A site near Kilmelfort in Argyll preserves in one such heap thousands of flint chippings. But rather like the shell-heaps of Oban and Oronsay, size does not attest a large number of people. A single flint knapper could, and usually did, turn out hundreds of them in a matter of days. In less profusion, though by no means rare, small worked flints have been found in many places, even as far as Orkney. They were probably used as borers and to form the barbs and points of arrows. The small cores from which they were struck must have made excellent tools for scraping hides and skins. Mention of these tiny flints, or microliths, in a way completes the circle of this introductory chapter for in them can be seen a clear connection with a third continental group. They represent a different people from south-west France and neighbouring parts of Europe and confirm our earliest conclusion that the nomads who penetrated into the Highlands and Islands from the seventh millennium B.C. onwards were by no means of a single identity.

It is probably true to say that, during a period twice as long as separates us from St Columba, they made no significant addition to the amenities of life which their ancestors had brought to the Highlands. One should not be surprised at this since, in general, it is not normally the nomadic peoples of any age who contribute startling innovations. Perhaps their prime achievement is that they used their resources to survive and to come to terms with an environment which at times must have seemed hostile in the extreme. How much longer their static way of life might have continued but for the external influences, is impossible to say. Presumably the changing climate played its part in the end. But it might have lasted immeasurably longer had not bands of strange immigrants appeared on the scene bringing with them new, revolutionary techniques and ideas.

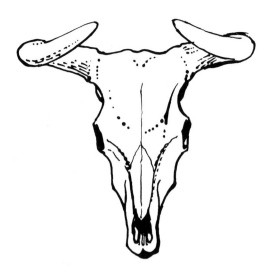

Livestock. A skull of *Bos primigenius*, the wild aurochs domesticated by neolithic man. Short-horned cattle were not kept in Britain until the Late Bronze Age. The long, scimitar-like horns of the bezoar, *Capra hircus aegagrus*, the earliest domesticated goat, developed the now characteristic ram's-horn twist very slowly during a long period of domestication. It still lives wild in the mountains of south-west Asia. The present-day Soay sheep of the Outer Hebrides are similar to the true mouflon, *Ovis musimon*, one of the three forms which once lived wild in Europe and Asia. Originally coarse haired its woolly fleece was the product of selective breeding in the earliest phases of its domestication.

The arrival of the new immigrants, perhaps about 4000 B.C., marks the beginning of the New Stone Age in the Highlands and Islands and the start of a new way of life, a settled, more or less stable, existence based on farming. Agriculture and the need for its organisation were major factors in the growth of the first cities—Eridu, Lagash, Uruk and, possibly the best known of all, Ur—and in the rise of the great metal-using civilisations of Sumer, Babylon and Egypt. If the results of its introduction into the Highlands and Islands seem somewhat less spectacular, first-farming was as important and significant here as elsewhere. It brought the radical change from the food-gathering of the nomadic, eskimo-like aborigines of whom there were perhaps no more than a dozen or so to a hundred square miles, to food-production by more numerous and numerically larger settled groups. At the same time, it laid the foundations of an economy that was to remain virtually unchanged, apart from technical and organisational improvements in the eighteenth century, until today.

Deliberate plant-raising and stock breeding had first been developed in the East several thousand years before while almost the whole of Britain lay under ice. By the time the glaciers had retreated to their present position, farming had already reached the Middle East. Agricultural implements found at Jericho date back at least to 9500 B.C. and, certainly by the end of that millennium, villagers over a wide area from Asia Minor to Iran and south to Israel were harvesting wheat and barley and tending flocks. From the Middle East farming continued to spread slowly westwards, first into Greece and later into Denmark until, eventually, land was being cultivated and cattle reared in almost all but the coldest places in Europe.

In the British Isles themselves the Neolithic Revolution, the introduction and spread of agriculture, took place in a surprisingly short period. Our first farmers were predominantly coastal dwellers who were neither strangers to the sea nor unprepared for long sea journeys. Hugging the coastlines they came by boat up the relatively safe inshore routes of the Irish Sea as far as the Hebrides and the Great Glen.

They carried their seed grain with them and somehow they also succeeded in transporting their livestock, cattle, sheep and goats. Settling on land near the sea, they began their farming in a climate that was rather drier than at present with warm summers to ripen their wheat and barley and winters that were not particularly severe. Those who were travelling on found the Great Glen, an easy route as far as inland routes go. In its seventy miles there were only two or three places where for a mile or so the immigrants would have had to carry their goods and boats and drive their cattle overland. Its steep sides and frowning mountains, however, offered little encouragement for them to dawdle and none at all to settle. Further movement northwards from the north-east end of the Great Glen was by way of the east coast and from Caithness the experienced seamen-farmers brought their boats to Orkney and ultimately to Shetland.

Perhaps at first they found, as the earliest farmers did almost everywhere else, that they needed to do little more than fell trees and roughly clear the land. Their seed grain would germinate in season and flourish in the rich earth and when the soil deteriorated, when weeds grew in profusion and there were no new areas for convenient development, they would clear the stones and tree stumps more assiduously and cultivate their land more systematically. The technique of land-clearance by a simple slash and burn method used in the Middle East soon exhausted the soil and the farmers had to move quite frequently to new tracts of land. This movement and an expanding population account for the gradual spread of agriculture from the Mediterranean basin, up the Danube valley, and eventually to Britain. Our own first-farmers solved one of the basic problems of land clearance—an equation in which reward is set against effort—by choosing to settle not on the most fertile land but in those areas that today might be considered marginal. The most fertile soil produced the densest vegetation and the most trees and so required the longest time and the greatest effort to clear.

One eventual outcome of all the land and forest clearance, and of the need to work

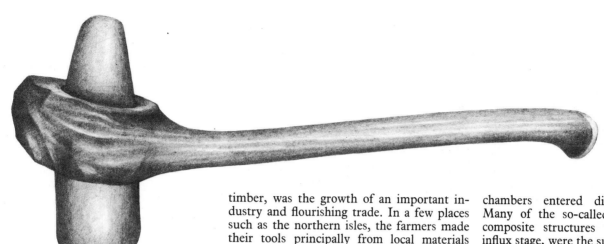

Polished axehead of greenish-grey volcanic tuff made at the Langdale, Lake District, factory. Recently, handles made of ash and copied from an original found in Sigerslev Bog, Denmark, were fitted with stone-age axeheads. Three men cleared 500 square metres of birch wood in four hours. One axehead, unsharpened since it was no doubt employed in similar work some four thousand years ago, was used to cut down a hundred trees. For some time after the start of the Neolithic Revolution in Britain both stone-age farmers and mesolithic hunter-fishers continued their own way of life and only very gradually did the latter come to assimilate the elements of the new economy. In this way the so-called Secondary Neolithic culture arose, represented in the North by such settlements as Skara Brae or by the stone axe factories.

timber, was the growth of an important industry and flourishing trade. In a few places such as the northern isles, the farmers made their tools principally from local materials but elsewhere in Britain the demand for axes led to the setting up of factories beside outcrops of suitably fine-grained rock. At these sites, chiefly Langdale in the Lake District, Craig Llwyd in north Wales and Tievebulliagh in Northern Ireland, tools were mass-produced and marketed either as rough blanks or as finished, ground and polished axeheads over most of Britain.

When the first farmers reached the Highlands and Islands, however, the industry had yet to grow. Their tools and implements like those of other pioneers were most probably reduced to a portable minimum of essentials. Nonetheless, the way in which they farmed their new land and husbanded their stock worked well enough for them. Supplemented by some food-gathering but more particularly by fishing, it would eventually not only provide for themselves and their rapidly increasing numbers but also produce occasional surpluses which could support groups engaged on activities completely outside the vital production of food: activities such as the building of the large-stone structures, the chambered tombs, through which they would make manifest to all their sense of community, identity and religious beliefs.

Two basic types of tomb can be distinguished amongst an apparently endless variety: 'passage graves' with chambers placed centrally in the cairns and entered, as the name implies, through a passage; and long, sometimes 'horned' cairns with gallery-like chambers entered directly from outside. Many of the so-called 'gallery graves' are composite structures which, after a short influx stage, were the subject of successive re-buildings over a very long period. The elements of their structures seem to have been combined and re-combined within an overall tradition, not the result of countless invaders each imposing their own special concepts, but of a continued local development of the basic religious theme by proud, peaceful communities for whom the monument was all important. Possibly there are close parallels in Christianity: a church enlarged or altered to meet the need for more space or to accommodate variations in the liturgy and, just as it is difficult to find two identical cathedrals, so one rarely finds two identical tombs.

Many of these very numerous monumental, large-stone structures were built in Scotland long before the pyramids of Egypt. They took the form of collective or communal tombs, an ancient equivalent, perhaps, of our family vaults, and were used for successive burials over many generations. In some, it first appeared that the most recent burial was left for a decent interval before being disrespectfully swept aside to make room for the next. In others, the several re-buildings of the chamber indicated another form of multiple burial and yet others possessed side chambers and recesses apparently for extra burials. Excarnation was probably a common feature of the burials and the dead were not placed in the tombs directly but first left exposed to the elements, or possibly buried away from the tomb before later exhumation and final interment in it.

Professor Colin Renfrew has depicted a view of life in the northern isles around 3000 B.C. that could be applied more generally. Orkney, he suggests, was at that time a mosaic of small communities, each of perhaps no more than twenty people, autonomous groups independent of one another yet enjoying close relations with neighbours. The chambered cairn of the territorial group was not the last resting place of distinguished chiefs or important individuals for there was no social stratification and each member of the egalitarian community, except infants, would be buried there when death came. Unfortunately, Renfrew's excavations at Quanterness apart, most of our information about burial rituals comes from individual inhumations of a slightly later date than that of the tombs' earliest users.

If the first farmers and tomb builders entered the Highlands and Islands by the western, coast-hugging route, the earliest tombs should be found in the south-west, in Argyll and on Arran and Bute and here, in fact, one does find simple, small rectangular chambers covered by modest cairns of a kind appropriate to pioneers. They are of various ground plans: some were closed and had porch-like elements in front; other chambers were open, sometimes long and narrow in proportion. Versions of this general type are found all around the Irish Sea coasts, in England and in the Pyrenees and Scandinavia.

In the Hebrides where there is an unusually uniform grouping of tombs, the dominant architecture is that of the polygonal passage grave. The normal chamber is round or oval, undivided, and covered usually by a round cairn ringed with kerbing stone and sometimes recessed to form a funnel-shaped forecourt. The same basic plan is found on Orkney, in Cromarty and, in fact, in so many places outside the Highlands and Islands that it is most probably the early form from which subsequent and more elaborate structures were developed. The Hebridean tombs are scattered but their centre appears to be on the more fertile island of North Uist where there is a remarkable concentration of them.

They are built principally inland on the once rich, undulating, upland pastures; in places

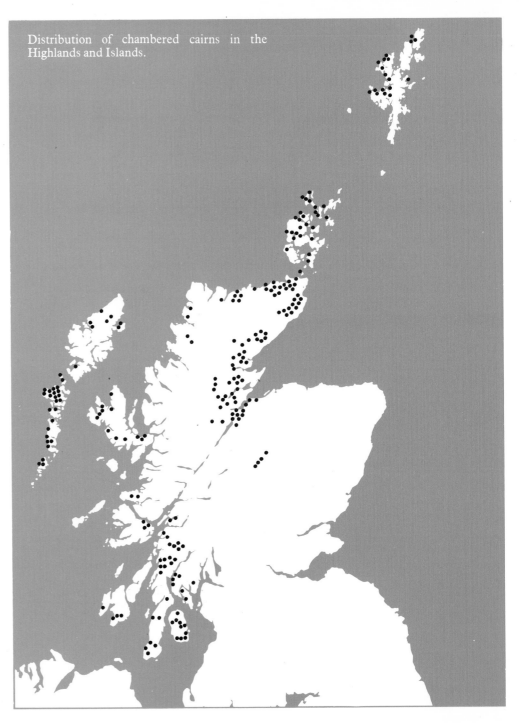

Distribution of chambered cairns in the Highlands and Islands.

An apparently endless variety of chambered
and unchambered cairns.

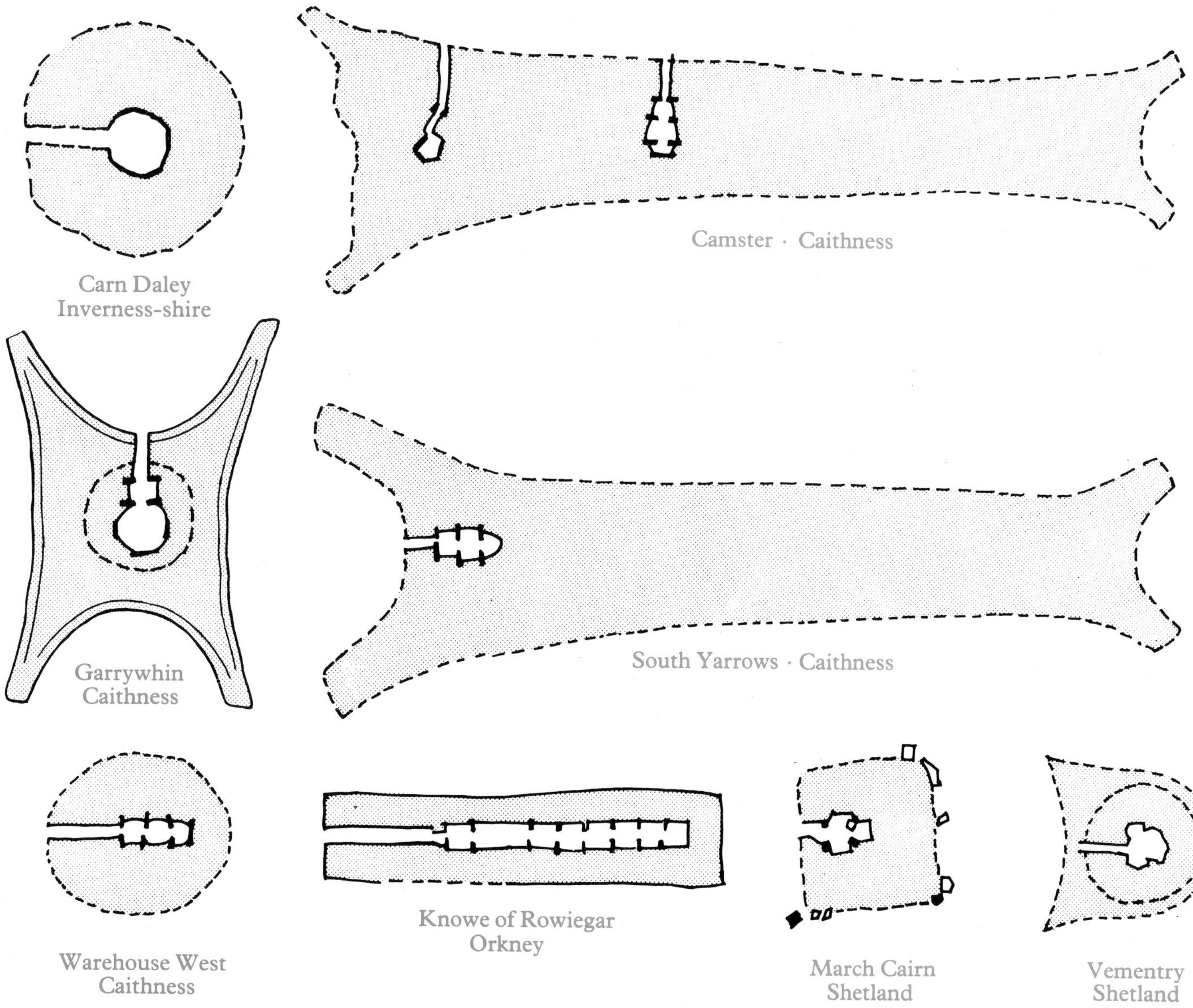

Carn Daley
Inverness-shire

Camster · Caithness

Garrywhin
Caithness

South Yarrows · Caithness

Warehouse West
Caithness

Knowe of Rowiegar
Orkney

March Cairn
Shetland

Vementry
Shetland

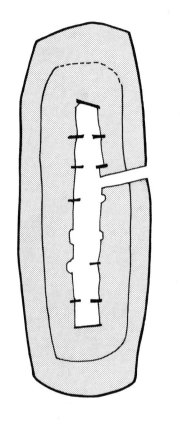

The stalled chamber of the neolithic cairn
of Blackhammer on Rousay

like Unival, where possibly the earliest of these tombs has been found, and Clettraval, both of which sites had a long occupation; much later Iron Age folk were to farm there and the remains of buildings scarcely more than a century old may be seen on the still-green, former summer shielings.

Unival, one of only four Hebridean tombs covered by square cairns, was excavated by Sir Lindsay Scott in the 1930's. He found that most of one side of the small chamber was occupied by a cist-like structure in which were the remains of the articulated skeleton of a mature woman surrounded by charcoal. 'Though much destroyed by fire these bones had not been cremated and their condition must be due to the piling of burning charcoal on them as they lay in the cist. Since it would be impracticable to light and maintain a substantial fire in so cramped and ill-ventilated a spot, the charcoal must have been brought into the tomb already burning and tipped out upon the cist. Even so, the heat generated would not have sufficed to consume the flesh and heavily to burn the bone within; we must therefore suppose that the flesh was already decayed when the burning took place . . . Presumably the bringing in of fire constituted the last stage of the funerary ritual, and was designed to drive the ghost away from its then decomposed body, and from the tomb, in order that it might take its departure to the place appropriate to disembodied spirits. It may also be inferred that the removal of the bones from the cist did not take place at this stage, but later, at the beginning of a new funerary cycle.' But if Unival, like other individual tombs, had such a long and complex history as is supposed, the elaborate ritual reconstructed by Sir Lindsay Scott and any of its associated finds would probably not be those of the original builders.

The group of cairns at the north-east end of the Great Glen, that geological fault which provided a main route for many immigrants, demonstrates an intense settlement by neolithic tomb-builders. Unfortunately their monuments have suffered severely here, principally as a result of the agricultural improvements of the eighteenth and nineteenth centuries when very many were removed

without trace. Generally speaking they differ from other cairns by being built on low-lying land, even—as at Corrimony, and Clava which gives its name to the group—on the flood plains of rivers. At Clava, sometimes referred to as a cemetery, seven or eight were built on a three-quarters of a mile stretch of the narrow valley floor of the River Nairn and three of these, at Balnuaran of Clava, are so closely sited as to touch one another. Two different but closely related structures were in use at roughly the same time: ring cairns with no passage and an open central area, and passage graves of the earliest, purest form. The similarity of the former to Spanish ring cairns and the classical simplicity of the latter, which is so close to that of Iberian sites, have led to the suggestion that the neolithic people who settled the Clava area came, not by the main west coast route and via the Great Glen, but more directly from south-west France and Spain, through Brittany and across the North Sea.

Owing to the destruction of so many cairns in this area, no new evidence is likely to be revealed by further field study, whereas in Orkney more is being learned almost annually about the tombs and about the life of the Neolithic Islanders. The recently excavated cairn of Quanterness is thought to have been built in about 3400 B.C. and to have continued in use until 2450 B.C. Here, Professor Colin Renfrew found a disordered scatter of human bones undisturbed for four and a half thousand years. They were the incomplete, disarticulated skeletal remains of bodies which had first been buried, and decomposed, elsewhere. All in all it is thought that the bones of four hundred people were placed in the tomb, of whom only a mere seven per cent had lived beyond the age of thirty. In the later stages of the tomb's use, c.2400 B.C., a body had been buried in an extended position whilst the much earlier remains (c.2900) of individual crouched burials were found in a cist and in several stone covered pits dug into the floor of the main chamber.

But Quanterness and the similar tomb of Quoyness on Sanday appear about the middle of the evolutionary sequence which Professor Renfrew traced in Orkney. If the earliest are

Balnuaran of Clava, NE. The simple circular chamber and entrance passage from the south. Beyond the round, kerbed cairn is a free standing circle of monoliths. The suggestion is that the construction of cairns, or artificial hills, for the 'houses of the dead' derives originally from the use of caves in natural hills as burial chambers.

19

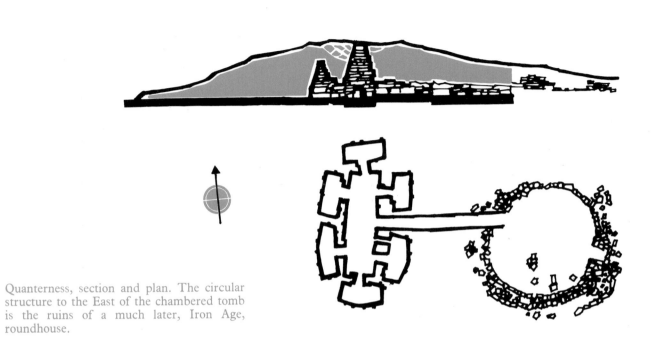

Quanterness, section and plan. The circular structure to the East of the chambered tomb is the ruins of a much later, Iron Age, roundhouse.

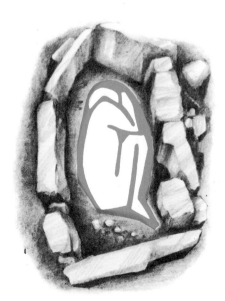

Left
A dense jumble of disarticulated human bones undisturbed for nearly five thousand years.

Centre
Cist cut into the floor of the main chamber at Quanterness. Fragments of skull found on the floor suggests the possibility of a crouched burial.

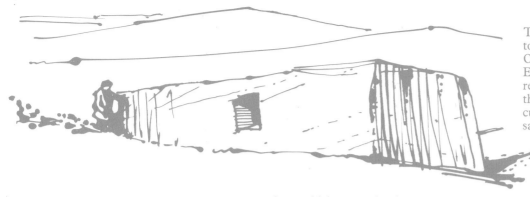

The device of cutting back into the hillside to form a level floor for the chamber of some Orcadian tombs was taken further at Calf of Eday, elaborated at Taversoe Tuik and reached its ultimate in the Dwarfie Stane on the Island of Hoy where the whole tomb is cut into the solid stone of a large block of old sandstone.

Bigland Round, Orkney.

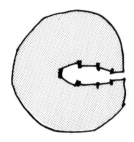

Warehouse South, Caithness.

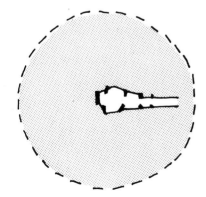

Among the earliest Orcadian tombs are those resembling larger structures in Caithness; a not surprising similarity if Orkney was settled, as one supposes, from the mainland.

those which most closely resemble tombs in Caithness, whence came the first Orcadian settlers, the small tripartite chambered cairns of Sandyhill Smithy on Eday and Bigland Round on Rousay would come near the start of the sequence. Later, on the small island of Rousay, the dominant architecture was to become that of the 'stalled' cairn in which long narrow chambers were divided into 'stalls' for the dead by upright flags of stone. On mainland Orkney a passage-grave development is seen from Unstan to the Quanterness group and finally to that outstanding monument of the superb skills of Orcadian masons, Maes Howe.

Almost everything about Maes Howe is remarkable—size, construction and structural detail. Its size suggests that it was the impressive centre not of one but of a number of the small egalitarian communities; which in turn implies the growth of some measure of central organisation. The enormous stones used in its construction which run the length of the fifteen-foot chamber, or the even longer monoliths which form the roof, sides and floor of the inner part of the passage, are positioned with accuracy and skilfully set and underpinned. The roof is a corbelled barrel-vault, formed in the tradition of the Orcadian craftsmen by oversailing one stone beyond the one beneath it until the walls almost met and could be capped at the top; but in its lower courses the stones were cleverly fractured at an obtuse angle so that the oversailing forms a smooth curve.

Parties of Vikings entered the tomb by way of the roof on several occasions in the twelfth century A.D. To them howe-breaking seems to have been a manly sport, both a test of courage and a treasure hunt. They left a series of twenty-four runic inscriptions on the walls, three of which refer to treasure: ' . . . great treasure was carried off in the course of three nights' . . . 'away to the north a great treasure is hidden' . . . 'Hakon single-handed bore treasure from this howe . . .'; but if such riches ever existed outside the minds of the graffitists, they were not left there by the early users of the tomb. Part of the bank which surrounds the cairn was, it is thought, reinforced about A.D. 900 and so, if the howe-breakers were telling the truth, perhaps the great treasure consisted of the golden grave goods from a Norse burial two centuries earlier.

By contrast the neolithic cairns of Shetland are small—some of them must be amongst the smallest chambered tombs anywhere—but, because they are sited on hills and knolls they are nonetheless conspicuous in a barren landscape. There is little arable land today; the summers are short and the islands are lashed by ferocious gales, but the climate is softened by warm sea currents, and cultivation, with oats and barley as the principal crops, was once important in the economy of the islands. Some of the fifty-seven or so neolithic tombs there have round cairns; the majority, however, belong to that distinctive Shetland type called 'heel-shaped' cairns. The chambers are either trefoil or rectangular in plan and the two forms seem to be about equal in number.

Storms and ferocious gales are not, of course, confined to Shetland. The Islands of Orkney 21 have their share and two of them, one revealing the other catastrophic in its effects, are of particular interest. In December 1824 a storm of exceptional severity stripped grass and sand from Skara Brae, a high dune by the Bay of Skaill on the west coast of Orkney mainland. When the storm had subsided a large midden heap and the ruins of ancient buildings were exposed, probably for the first time in more than four thousand years. They proved eventually to be part of a prehistoic settlement, a complex of stone houses and connecting passages built and then re-built between about 3100 B.C. and 2450 B.C. by groups of stone-age pastoralists.

The site as the visitor sees it today represents principally the second of two main building phases and the later period of occupation when at least six houses were in use. Each is roughly square in plan with rounded corners. The dry-stone walls, some of them 1.2 metres thick, corbelled inwards for a few courses at the top, especially at the corners, and supported a solid timber, turf-covered roof left open in the centre to form a smoke-hole. The several houses were each entered by tunnel-like passages and small doorways on average about 1.1 m high by 0.6 m wide. Immediately inside the doorways on either side are holes designed to hold the bar that fastened the door in place.

In the centre of each house is a square hearth framed by stones and against each of two opposing walls is a bed, a boxlike stone structure with tall stone 'bedposts' to support a canopy. The bed on the right as one enters is always the larger of the two even in the earlier buildings in which beds of the same design were set into the walls themselves. Immediately above the beds are handy recesses or open cupboards for the personal possessions of the occupants of the beds below who slept on 'mattresses' made of bundles of heather covered with animal skins. The beds were probably the nearest approach to privacy that any individual could attain in the communal, 'open-plan' dwellings and they were places in which to hide special things, a fine bead necklace or a choice joint saved from the last meal. Against the rear wall of each house stands a curious piece of stone furniture, a

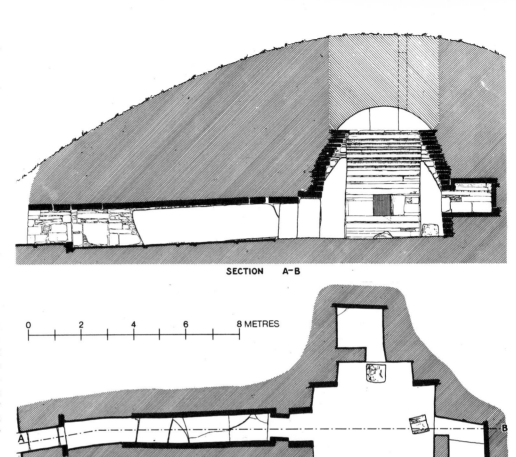

SECTION A–B

PLAN

C.S.T.CALDER

Maes Howe, section and plan. Nomads like the earlier mesolithic seldom took much trouble over the burial of their dead. When people began to live in settled communities, however, the dead were usually carefully interred; eventually in some later Neolithic and Early Bronze Age communities it became the practice to place food and drink, tools, weapons and prized personal possessions in the grave with the body. No such grave goods nor rich treasure from the neolithic users of the tomb awaited the Vikings who broke into Maes Howe in the mid twelfth century A.D.

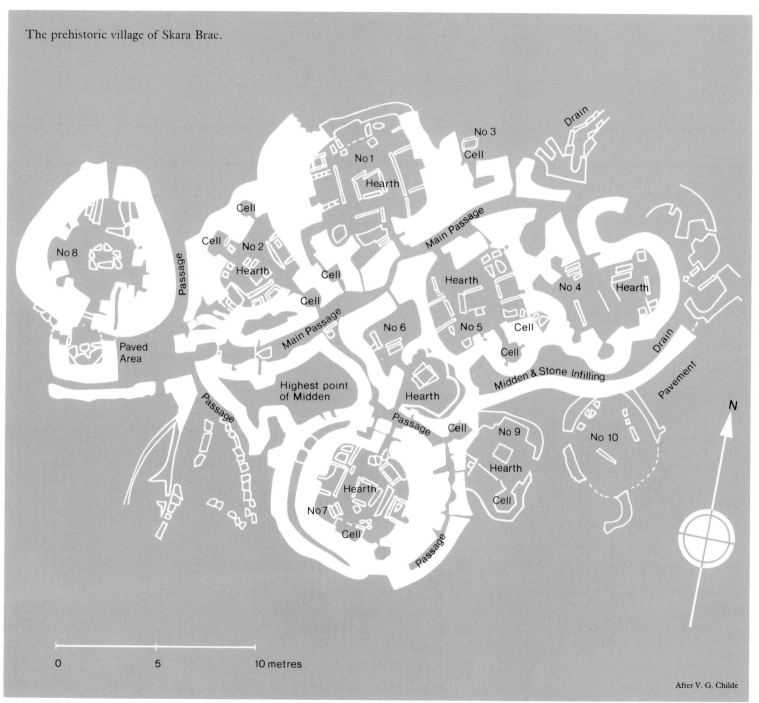

The prehistoric village of Skara Brae.

Drain

No 3
Cell

No 1
Hearth

Cell
Main Passage

Cell
Cell
No 2
Hearth
Cell
Cell
Main Passage

No 8

Paved
Area

Passage

Hearth
No 4
Hearth

No 6
No 5
Cell
Cell

Highest point
of Midden

Hearth

Midden & Stone Infilling

Drain
Pavement

Passage

Passage
Cell

No 9
Hearth
Cell

No 10

No 7
Cell
Cell

Passage

N

0   5   10 metres

After V. G. Childe

23

two-storied cupboard, the equivalent of the modern dresser. Let into the floor in a corner are three or more boxes formed by slate slabs and sealed with clay at the joints to make them watertight.

The villagers had been cattle breeders first and foremost from the time they settled at Skara Brae, although in the latter part of their occupation they increased their flocks of sheep and goats and perhaps kept a few pigs. They worked their dogs not so much in hunting deer, for they ate little venison, but as cattlemen have always done to guard their flocks and herds from predators. The prime supplement to their main diet of beef and mutton was flesh. Limpet shells appear in large quantities in their middens as they do at many prehistoric sites.

Some shells were used as small dishes to hold decorative earth pigments such as ochre, while the flesh of the limpet was removed from the shell and soaked in clean water in those tanks set into the floor. Here the hard rim round the flesh softened until it was fit to bait the 'hooks', gorges made of splinters of bone or wood, for the bottom-feeding cod and coalfish. The presence of more than one tank in each house, thus allowing them to be used in rotation, underlines the importance of fishing and demonstrates the prudence of the villagers in keeping a ready supply for use in those months when other bait was scarce.

Apart from limpets some edible shellfish such as crabs were gathered for food and the humble winkle was not ignored; its shells could be pierced and used as beads. Birds' eggs, too, were collected and, although the birds themselves formed only a small part of the diet, if indeed they were eaten at all, they were nonetheless important to the community. Almost all the awls, essential piercing tools since skins and hides were the only 'fabrics', were made from the bones of birds like the gannet.

As coastal dwellers, possibly with a long tradition of seamanship behind them, the villagers looked more to the sea than the land for provisions. Quantities of carbonised grain were found in the middens of early settlers but very little in later ones and so far nothing has yet come to light to show that any of them cultivated the land around Skara Brae. But the sea was more than a larder: it brought them pieces of pumice eroded from outcrops in Iceland to shape their bone pins and awls and, more important by far in their virtually treeless landscape, it left large quantities of driftwood on the shores, not simply small branches to fashion into handles for tools but spruce trees of considerable size ·from the great virgin forests of North America which they could shape and bind with ropes twisted from heather to form their roofing timbers. The sea's bounty was, however, uncertain. Perhaps this is why the settlers chose to make their furniture of stone; possibly they were not confident of their carpentry, while the eminently suitable local stone was there in plenty and could be worked by them with apparently skilful ease. Their furniture and many of their structures have endured for some four thousand years, surviving—if not wholly intact—the catastrophe which abruptly brought the long occupation of the settlement to an end.

Doubtless another violent storm set the nearby dunes in motion and caused them to envelop the village with alarming suddenness. Everything points to a very hurried evacuation. One woman in her frantic haste to leave broke her necklace while squeezing through the narrow doorway of her house and scattered the beads along a passageway as she ran. Treasured possessions, some laboriously and ingeniously fashioned or in the process of being made, were abandoned where they lay; small cups of shell and whalebone containing red, yellow and blue pigments for body painting, bone pendants, pins and awls, fine necklaces, stone axes and knives, flint tools and those curious carved stone balls. A small group of people visited the sand-choked settlement after the storm had subsided, lit a fire in the lee of the broken walls and prepared a meal of shellfish and venison. If it was a party of the now homeless villagers, they would have found little to comfort them in their loss, for their houses and possessions were buried almost a metre deep in sand.

Skara Brae stone furniture

A two-tiered "dresser"

Interior of House No 1

Floor tanks in which limpet flesh was soaked for bait appear in both drawings

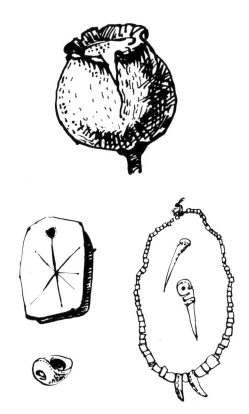

The puff-ball, *Bovista nigrescens*, in its adult fruit form was collected by the inhabitants of Skara Brae. Amongst a variety of uses, its cottonwool-like inside tissue was used to staunch bleeding wounds and help the blood to clot on small cuts.

A bone pendant about 26 mm long; pierced winkle shell used as a bead; a necklace of the type which the woman broke in her haste to leave House No. 7 on the night of the catastrophic storm which terminated the long occupation of Skara Brae.

'Main Street', Skara Brae, one of the passage-ways.

Amongst the strange objects left by the evacuees from Skara Brae are a number of carved stone objects, possibly implements of some kind, and highly decorative stone balls whose purpose is a mystery.

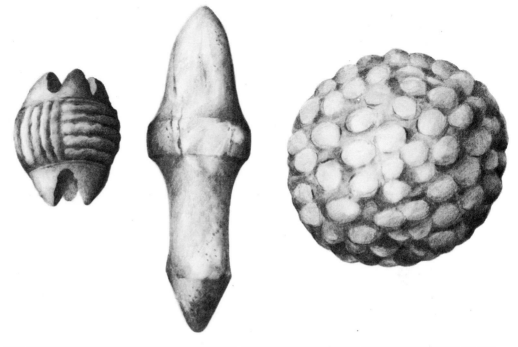

Pottery and potsherds are one of the most useful types of artifact from an archaeologist's point of view. They are almost indestructible and even quite small pieces can provide information about a period or culture from the type of decoration on them or by their composition and form. The craft was once thought to be an achievement of neolithic peoples but there are places—Sudan, Kenya and Denmark—where pottery antedates agriculture and others—Jericho and Anatolia—where the earliest farmers made no pottery at all.

The pottery used by the pastoralists of Skara Brae has the characteristic plant-pot shape, flat based with straight walls, of Grooved Ware, one of two distinct types associated with Middle and Late Neolithic peoples. It is often profusely decorated by incision, applied strips of clay and dots usually in geometrical patterns of triangles and lozenges. Although it was made and used over a wide area of southern Britain as well as at Skara Brae and Rinyo, it has been found in only two chambered tombs in the Highlands and Islands, Unival N. Uist and Tormore, Arran.

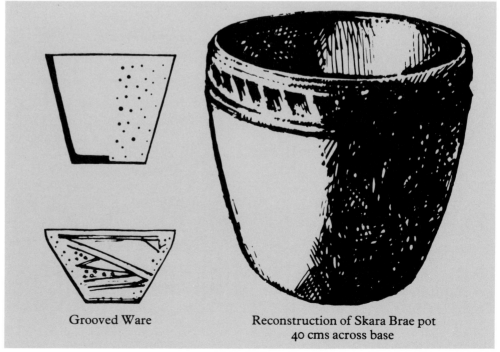

Grooved Ware

Reconstruction of Skara Brae pot
40 cms across base

27

Grooved Ware came into popular use about 3000 B.C., replacing after a transition period the earlier, typically round-based Unstan Ware.

Basic forms of Neolithic A, Primary or Western, pottery after Piggott. In the widest sense the greater part of the pottery of the chambered tombs of Scotland falls into this category. The uncarinated bowls, those with unridged, smooth profiles, were less affected by changes than the carinated ware, bowls with a pronounced ridge the junction of two different clay forms, which developed distinctive local styles.

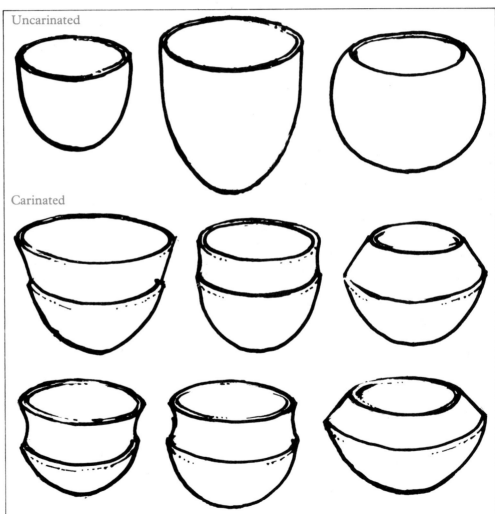

Uncarinated

Carinated

Both types were in use side by side as the paired bowls found at Beacharra in Argyll show.

Maths and Metals

Not long after Maes Howe was built, work began on two other remarkable structures, the henges of Brodgar and Stenness only a kilometre or so away. Most of the numerous henges and stone circles, ritual or ceremonial sites that are found only in the British Isles, date from about the same time; some thirty stone circles and seven henges have been discovered in the Highlands and Islands area alone. In physical terms henges differ from stone circles in that their circular site is defined by a ditch and bank but not all follow an identical plan. Some have a single causewayed entrance, others two opposing ones whilst Avebury in southern England, the largest of all, has four. Many have additional features such as a centrally placed tomb and a ring of standing stones or timber posts. Avebury, Stonehenge and Woodhenge are perhaps the best known of all these numerous monuments but there are two in the Highlands and Islands, the Ring of Brodgar on Orkney and the Standing Stones of Callanish on Lewis, that are no less impressive. Recent surveys at these and many other sites suggest that we may have to revise our long-held views of middle and late stone age man and our concept of Britain as a distant outpost of civilisation, reacting belatedly to changes and advances made in the Near and Middle East.

Perhaps the stones of the henges and circles do simply signify a ritual area, or a place of assembly for a society for whom the sacred and secular were inextricably mixed. Professor Alexander Thom, amongst the latest and most painstaking of those who have investigated these monuments, proposes a more scientific interpretation of their signifiance. His tentative conclusions suggest that late neolithic man in these islands was capable of quite complex geometrical and astronomical thought. Stone circles and groups of standing stones are planned to satisfy geometrical criteria. Some of the stone circles have a true circle plan, others are laid out as ellipses and in some the circle has been flattened along part of its perimeter with the result that the ratio of the circumference to diameter is 3:1 and not π, or 3.14159:1. The axes, diameters and perimeters were often measured in the same standard unit, the 'Megalithic Yard',

0.829 m, which in some way the builders were able to apply with consistent accuracy— Thom calculates an accuracy of 1 in 1,000 — through the whole of Britain. How, or through what agency, the megalithic engineers achieved this is not known, but it cannot have been easy without some form of central organisation.

Groups of stones within the circles or placed as outliers near them are set in a way which suggests they would have made admirable astronomical sighting devices. Some stones align with points on the horizon where the sun, moon or stars rise and set at significant times in their orbits, events which can have great importance to a farming people. Observations of the sun and the identification of the summer and winter solstices (21 June and 21 December) and the spring and autumn equinoxes (21 March and 21 September), provide the basis for an accurate calendar which the stone circle users could sub-divide into sixteen 'months', or more simply still into the vital seasons.

Stonehenge lies in a position that is particularly suitable for solar and calendaric calculations; Callanish, however, was built at a significant latitude for lunar observations. The moon appears to skim the southern horizon for a few days every eighteen and a half years. At these times it rises a few degrees east and sets a few degrees west of south while a short distance further north it does not rise at all. Professor Thom suggests that the Callanish folk not only knew about this 18.61 year lunar cycle, the time it takes the moon, rotating on its monthly orbits, to move away from and return to the same relative position in the heavens, but that they also discovered the wobble of about nine minutes of arc in the orbit. With such an intimate knowledge of the moon's celestial movements, it would have been possible to predict with some accuracy eclipses—those awesome if not terrifying events.

In the centre of the ring of standing stones at Callanish a single monolith almost five metres high has been placed and it was noticed many years ago that anyone standing on a natural outcrop to the south, and looking along the

Henge monuments and stone circles in the
Highlands and Islands. The physical difference between henges and circles is that the
ritual area of the henge is delineated by a
ditch. The lintel or hanging stone which gives
these sites their name is only to be found at
Stonehenge.

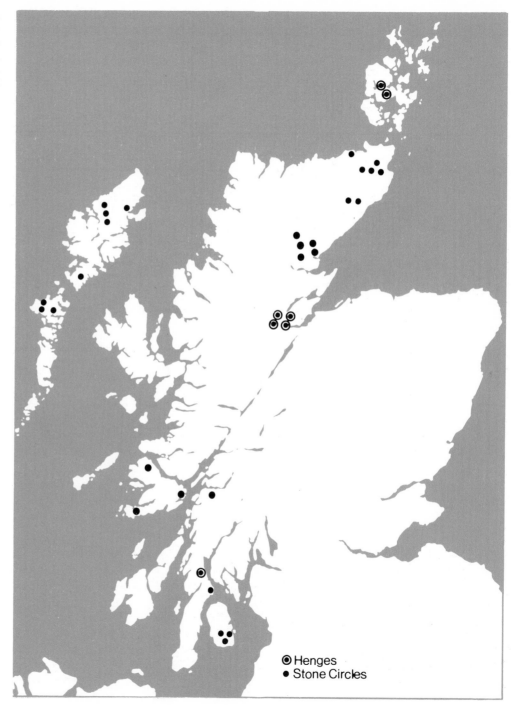

⊙ Henges
● Stone Circles

31

The stone ring at Callanish, with the chambered cairn, showing the suggested geometry of the flattened circle which Professor A. Thom calls Type A. Other sites may have a true circle plan like Brodgar, yet others elliptical ones.

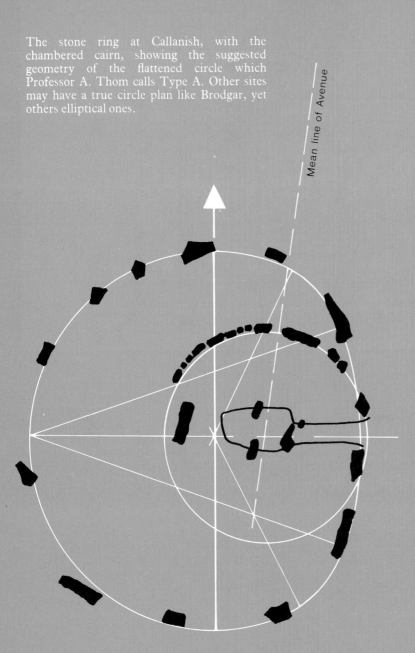

Mean line of Avenue

Plan of the Callanish Stones

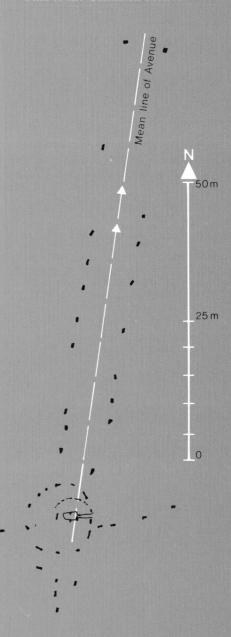

Mean line of Avenue

N

50 m

25 m

0

As Stonehenge lies on a latitude particularly good for solar observations, Callanish is especially well sited for observing the moon.

Every 18.61 years the moon skims less than 2° above the southern horizon at Callanish. In 55 B.C. the Greek historian Diodorus might have been describing Lewis when he wrote of an island he called Hyperborea with its round temple from which the moon appears but little distance from the earth every nineteen years.

Among the important sightlines distinguished by Professor Thom is the mid-summer full moonset at Mt Clisham as seen from Callanish and the moon crossing the notch formed by the cliffs at Helia, Hoy, one of at least three sights which could have been used by megalithic astronomers at the Ring of Brodgar.

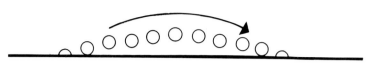

The 'Moon skim' at Callanish

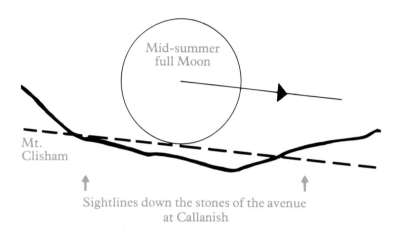

Mid-summer full Moon

Mt. Clisham

Sightlines down the stones of the avenue at Callanish

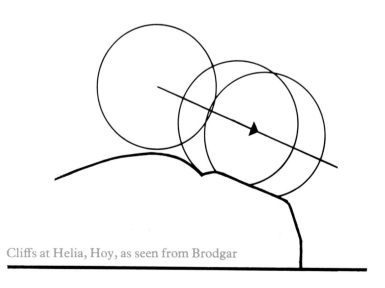

Cliffs at Helia, Hoy, as seen from Brodgar

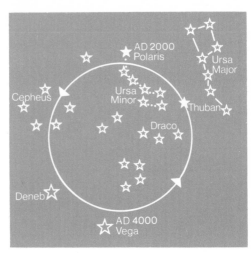

The Earth is not a perfect sphere, it is flattened at the poles and it bulges at the equator (the diameter through the poles is about 42 km less than the equatorial diameter). Heavenly bodies, particularly the sun and moon exert a pull on the equatorial bulge causing the earth to wobble on its axis or precess. The effect of precession is seen in the change of the earth's pole star. For neolithic man the north star was Thuban in the constellation Draco; in 12,000 years time it will be Vega, the bright star in Lyra.

line of stones that forms the head of the cross could see the Pole Star directly above the central pillar on a clear night. These stones are aligned due north, in fact, although it was not Polaris, our Pole Star, but Thuban in the constellation Draco which indicated north when the late stone age builders established its direction so accurately. To the left, the arm of the cross points a few degrees off due west, but nevertheless sunset at the spring and autumn equinoxes still occurs very close to this alignment; so why do neither the long avenue nor the eastern arm indicate north and east in a cardinal symmetry that was obviously within the capacity of the builders to achieve?

One theory is that the long avenue was a Processional Way with ritual rather than astronomical significance and, looking south down this double row of standing stones towards the centre of the circle, it is not difficult to see how such an idea arose. Rear Admiral Boyle T. Somerville who prepared a detailed plan of the site in 1912 thought that the avenue aligned with the rising of the bright star Capella in the north and that the eastern arm indicated the Pleiades while in 1963 Professor Gerald Hawkins, an American astronomer, concluded that the same eastern arm pointed to the setting of the equinoctial moon.

All in all the late neolithic builders of these megaliths appear to have possessed a knowledge which is surprisingly advanced for their time and place. As farming folk, obviously they needed to know when to cultivate the land and when to plant their seed grain, but far simpler observations would have sufficed. Equally obviously, they had through their farming and building traditions practical experience in field engineering, but their pre-occupation with geometry, with integral lengths and perimeters, and their use of Pythagorean triangles long before Pythagoras propounded his elegant Theorem, implies a depth and breadth of knowledge hitherto unrecognised. It also suggests that the complex neolithic society in Britain contained innovators of practices and concepts antedating those of the Mediterranean cultures.

In the Late Neolithic period (c.2500 B.C.) new groups of people arrived in Britain to enjoy an initial period of superiority and a long co-existence with the earlier settlers. They introduced a number of innovations, one of which was their distinctive style of pottery, a decided contrast with neolithic ware, graceful and subtly curved, fine red ware, proportionately tall and narrow, richly decorated with clearly organised bands of incised geometric patterns, and known to us as 'beakers' because of its handle-less drinking-cup form. Such exotic pottery became widespread over Europe, from Ireland to Hungary and from Norway to Morocco with particular concentrations along the Atlantic Coasts. The origins of the Beaker people themselves, however, are uncertain. They have been placed as far apart as Iberia and Eastern Europe and, in the more immediate sense as the source of the British settlements, in the Rhine basin. For some time after their arrival they appear to have remained somewhat aloof from the native population, but they did assimilate, here as elsewhere on the Continent, many aspects of local culture, farming practice, ritual and religion and, possibly, domestic architecture. In exchange they brought metallurgy, their distinctive pottery and possibly textiles, a new concept of burial and a range of new equipment. They were skilled engineers and surveyors and made their special contribution to local ritual architecture. They brought new social concepts, too, political power, and the organisation of society by stratification.

One of the places in which they settled in the Highlands was the Crinan Plain of Argyll where they made use of one of the earlier chambered tombs at Nether Largie and where traces of an even earlier activity had been left by mesolithic flint knappers. In this fertile valley there were copper deposits close to the seaways to gold-bearing Ireland and the tin of Cornwall, and near to the pass which led eastwards to the new communities of the Tay Valley. There was rich farming land and a climate, warmer and drier than the region enjoys today, to encourage their crops. The extent to which their initial settlement involved working together with the local groups is problematic, but they were clearly present on the site for a long time. Eventually they

Many cup-and-ring marks that are usually associated with the Beaker folk are to be found in Argyll. Carved with a pick or perhaps a hammer and chisel they have been variously interpreted as sun symbols, sources of heat, and as marks peculiar to metal workers.

built a linear cemetery over a total distance of almost five kilometres to the north and south of the approximately central cairn.

There is nothing anywhere in Scotland quite like this long, linear cemetery. Its cists contain end slabs let into grooves suggesting, as Professor Stuart Piggott has remarked, carpenters' techniques transferred to stone. Some of the grave lids are decorated with examples of Highland graphic art that probably rank amongst the most vivid. The northernmost cairn has carvings of axe-heads and a stone cover is pecked with forty-one cup marks belonging to the tradition of cup-and-ring decoration in stone associated with the Beaker people but whose significance is still a matter of lively speculation. Since they appear to a large extent where there are gold and copper deposits, as in the Kilmartin area of Argyll where large rock surfaces are decorated, it has been suggested that they may in some way bear relation with metal, its extraction and working. Such designs, however, may have derived from an earlier time and, enigmatic though they be, there is in them a hint of connections not only with Ireland and south-west England, but also further afield, with Brittany and the Iberian Peninsula.

The Beaker folk are generally regarded as people who did not follow the communal or cremation burial practices of the egalitarian stone-using native population amongst whom they settled, but who buried their important dead individually with legs flexed or drawn right up in a crouched posture. There are exceptions; cremations are known though they are not common in Britain, and two or more bodies were sometimes placed in graves. Richly decorated beakers usually accompanied the dead though none was found in the cist on the Isle of Arran which otherwise yielded a rare find—a metal dagger with gold mountings. But perhaps the living were unwilling as a rule to part with objects so rare and precious before they could be manufactured locally. Almost five hundred years were to elapse after the arrival of the Beaker folk in the Late Neolithic period before bronze working was developed and then only after a copper-working phase which yielded tanged knives and daggers with their beaker and central

European connections, and flat axes and those curious weapons, halberds, which in essence were simply daggers mounted at right angles to their shafts, concentrated for the most part in Ireland.

In south-eastern Europe people had learned to extract and smelt copper and to make implements and ornaments from it well before 4000 B.C. Perhaps many of the implements were themselves ornamental since they were no more durable, nor easier to make, than similar artifacts of stone. Rather later—it may have been in the second city of Troy—a technical break-through was made with the discovery that if copper and tin are melted together in the proportion of about 8:1 the less brittle alloy we call bronze is formed. When the effects of this discovery reached the Highlands and Islands about 2000 B.C., the Bronze Age began there.

Little is known of the domestic life of the Early Bronze Age people except from such settlements as Northton in Harris and Stanydale in Shetland. Here, on this latter site, people were to continue to use locally available stone for tools when metal was normal in other parts of Scotland; an early example of the economic difficulties that have faced the northern and the western isles throughout history.

The artistic taste of the Early Bronze Age women expressed itself in personal adornments, some obtained from afar, others home-made. There are the basket-shaped ear ornaments found at Migdale in Sutherland which resemble a gold pair from Orton in Moray, the pair of bracelets of decorated bronze plate preserved at Melfort in Argyll and, most intricate of all, the necklaces of jet beads. These necklaces are largely a Scottish device and are closely associated with lunulae, chest ornaments made from crescent-shaped sheets of beaten gold by Early Bronze Age craftsmen in Ireland and Scotland. Not only are the lunulae of similar shape and decorative purpose, but the raised or chased bead-like decoration seems to suggest that they may well have been copied from the jet necklace. Thirteen examples have so far come to light—one was discovered with a pair of cuff armlets 35

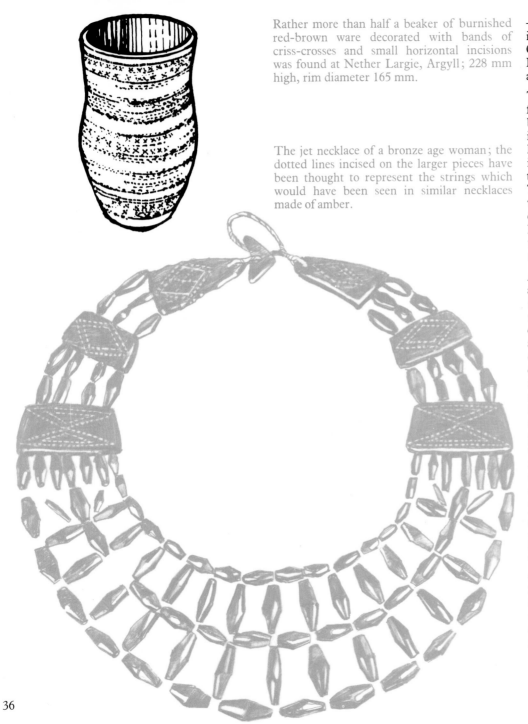

Rather more than half a beaker of burnished red-brown ware decorated with bands of criss-crosses and small horizontal incisions was found at Nether Largie, Argyll; 228 mm high, rim diameter 165 mm.

The jet necklace of a bronze age woman; the dotted lines incised on the larger pieces have been thought to represent the strings which would have been seen in similar necklaces made of amber.

—but possibly the most outstanding discovery is the burial hoard from the Knowes of Trotty, Orkney's largest concentration of Early Bronze Age graves, which contained part of an amber necklace and two gold 'sun' discs.

The last neolithic peoples and the Beaker folk themselves eventually became absorbed by the close of the Early Bronze Age. The innovative society, delicately balanced and hierarchical, the kind most susceptible to internal or external changes, was not destined to flourish much later than 1500 B.C. The remarkable stone circles and alignments were abandoned and presumably a store of engineering, mathematical and astronomical knowledge was lost with them, leaving us with the impression of a minor 'Dark Age', a trough between cultural peaks.

An invasion of the Highlands by a conquering aristocracy has been proposed, conjuring up an image of groups of dedicated materialists sweeping away the old order to found new communities; men whose fine bronze weapons and ornaments were passed on from parent to child and not buried in their graves. But no origin has been found for these 'newcomers' and, furthermore, the bronze industry of the earlier period continues without obvious interruption. Another sign of continuity is seen outside the Highland area at the important site of Cairnpapple in West Lothian, where the cremations of the new fashion were respectfully interred in the traditional type of cairn.

The main change after 1500 B.C. was religious. Diverse monuments associated with burials are rarely found. In the Early Bronze Age it is possible to distinguish between groups who buried their dead, or cremated them, or used both burial rites. From about 1500 B.C., cremation dominates the ritual. But changes in burial fashion are common through all ages. In Britain alone tastes have changed several times in the last two centuries for no obvious cultural reason. The rejection of the megaliths is far more profound, a change perhaps comparable to the abandonment of churches and cathedrals in modern times.

A plausible alternative to the 'armed invaders' theory is the idea of a deteriorating climate

Long after the late neolithic folk built their 'temple' at Stanydale in Shetland, early bronze age farmers there continued to use stone tools when metal was normal elsewhere in Britain.

The building is not a tomb nor is it the usual form of house. Because its plan is similar to that of the local 'heel-shaped' cairns it is thought to have had a religious function—hence 'temple'. The two post holes along its main axis once held spruce poles and since spruce is not native to Scotland these may well have drifted over from the vast coastal forests of America.

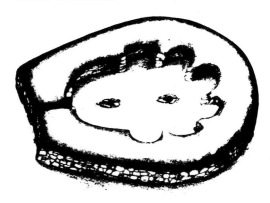

leading to profound economic change. Many of the megaliths were built on what was probably marginal land for cultivation. With the change in climate, the increased rainfall and a higher water-table, arable farming would have become less and less productive; indeed, the onset of peat growth round the outstanding monument of Callanish illustrates the risks which beset these sites. In addition, the recurrence of cloudier weather could have increased the problems of astronomical observation which, at the best of times, could never have been the easiest of tasks on the Atlantic coast. Though positive evidence of the climatic theory is still scanty, it is possible that an initial deterioration occurred about 1500 B.C., was followed by a period of poor weather, cloudier, wetter and colder than before, and culminated in a second more serious deterioration about 1100 to 1000 B.C.

Whatever the precise explanation for the cultural change at this time, the changed society soon became well adapted to the rigours of Highland life. A well developed bronze technology provided local farmers with tools for forest clearance and carpentry, whilst the womenfolk's attractive jewellery shows signs of Irish influence. Yet there are ominous signs of unrest in the background, as seen in the hoard of thirteen bronze rapiers found in Drumcoltran in south-west Scotland. Is this the stock of a travelling merchant supplying harassed communities or indeed the assembled armoury of such a group? Whilst many bronzes of this period are clearly status symbols, the gradual build-up of weaponry hints at an increase in inter-communal strife. The essentially peaceful rivalry inherent in the construction of a mightier chambered tomb or a more accurate megalithic observatory has been replaced by a more openly aggressive competition for status objects, for the finest available exotic articles and, most dangerous of all, for the most fertile arable and pasture lands. Clearly such competing groups would be alert to military innovations and watchful to gain advantage over their neighbours and rivals.

From about 1000 B.C. we find a radical transformation of arms, tools and ornaments throughout Britain. Although probably inspired by changes in Central Europe, the new weapons and tools passed through many local variations before their adoption in Scotland. As today, the offensive and defensive technologies interacted; thus, the innovation of the heavier slashing sword was balanced by the development of sheet bronze body armour. Hoards of weapons dating from the eighth century B.C. indicate that Scottish chieftains could command the services of specialist armourers.

Apart from the apparent 'arms race', local groups benefited from the far wider availability of bronze. Diverse tools—gouges, chisels, curved knives, hammers, anvil and razors—all became common. Tangible wealth is another mark of the age, perhaps indicated best by such fabulous hoards as the 36 gold armlets found on Islay.

Our best-preserved Bronze Age settlement has survived at Jarlshof on the southern tip of the Shetland mainland. Here, sometime after 1000 B.C., Bronze Age folk established a hamlet of stout stone dwellings surrounded by a light wall that extended right across the promontory. Six houses in all have been found, of which four relatively early ones are of the 'courtyard' type, oval in shape with a central hearth, a pair of cubicles on either side and a large transverse chamber at the inner end—a type of great antiquity in the islands, showing affinities to the design of neolithic chambered tombs. There was frequent rebuilding here, and it appears that no more than three houses were occupied on the site at any one time.

The inhabitants were farmers who grew barley around the settlement and bred Soay sheep, a large-horned breed whose descendants still survive amongst today's stock in Shetland. They also kept cattle of a breed related to the Celtic short-horn. They fished, particularly for cod, collected shellfish, and hunted seals and wildfowl. Basically theirs was a broad-based stone-age economy, drawing its amenities from local materials. Implements were fashioned of quartz and slate, stone and bone; pots were made of clay and steatite; there were heavy stone implements

Callanish

for quarrying and hoeing, slate shovels for arresting the inroads of sand.

It was not until about 600 B.C. that the first metal-worker appeared, a bronze smith who set up his workshop in a dwelling that had been abandoned. A cubicle to the east of the original entrance became his rubbish tip, and here have been found pieces of clay moulds for axes and swords, gouges and ornaments. The smith's dagger may offer a clue to his origins, for it is of Irish extraction: possibly he reached Jarlshof in the train of some chieftain.

Beside the villages of Shetland are other structures more in keeping with the social tensions of this increasingly warlike age. The most striking are the hill-forts, whose defences include some of the earliest known in Scotland: notably Dun Lagaidh built in about 560 B.C. in Wester Ross. Its rubble-packed wall was strengthened by a timber framework —a technique new to the Highland zone, though it had been used in the second city of Troy almost two thousand years before and was later favoured by the Gauls during Caesar's campaign against them. These timber-laced forts were highly susceptible to fire and many sites were destroyed either accidentally or deliberately in this manner, leaving the characteristic vitrified remains of stone fused with charcoal and wood-ash.

The origins of these and later fortifications probably relate to inter-communal pressures, whether direct population increase, or the territorial expansion of the stronger groups at the expense of the weaker. Another possibility is the threat of cattle-raiding. Whether local chieftains hired specialist fort-builders from the Continent or invented the new technique of timber-laced defences themselves is not clear, but henceforth defensive sites were to become the commonest monuments until the end of the Roman period.

The Celts

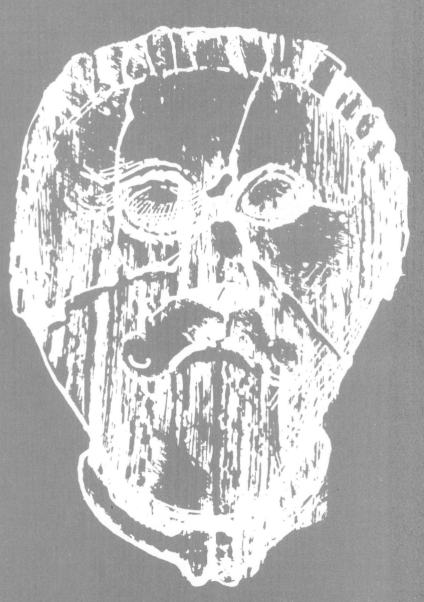

The climatic deterioration which has been suggested as a reason for the decline of the megalithic astronomers around the year 1500 B.C. is not clearly documented, but the same cannot be said for the onset of the climatic phase known as the Sub-Atlantic. All over Europe in the seventh century B.C. the levels of lakes rose, the lines of tree growth on high ground fell, and peat accumulated in many lowland areas. The Highlands and Islands on the rim of Europe were particularly exposed to this process, although the effects of the cooler and wetter weather on their inhabitants are difficult to assess precisely. However much agriculture suffered, ancient field systems have been discovered in large areas, evidence that it was not abandoned altogether.

About the same time a fresh impetus spread through the British Isles with the introduction of Late Bronze Age metal-working. This pre-historic industrial revolution is associated with the name of Hallstatt in Austria, where some graves were excavated in the 19th century that gave the name of their locality to what the archaeologists have since called the Hallstatt culture. Hallstatt traders, smiths and adventurers reached parts of Britain before 600 B.C. and in the following century a wave of settlement, essentially Hallstatt in character, reached its height. These immigrants introduced the manufacture and use of iron into Britain, and even if the first Celtic speakers here had been Beaker folk, it was these who filled the land with their dialects of the Celtic tongue. Before the end of the fifth century, when iron was known in most regions of Britain, the second period of the European Iron Age had succeeded to that of Hallstatt. It is named La Tène after a marvellous deposit of metalwork discovered in Switzerland, whose style is recognisable over a vast area from Ireland to Galatia, from the northern isles to the Pyrenees.

The term Celtic was first preserved in writing by the early Greeks, who used it to describe the barbaric peoples of central and west-central Europe as Keltoi. The identity thus conferred upon them is confirmed by the uniformity of their weapons and tools, ornaments and burial modes, and also by the common language-root upon which the definition of Celtic peoples is based. Naturally this branched into a variety of forms, just as the modern families of languages have done, and the most notable distinction is one that still exists between the Welsh and the Gaelic tongues. The peoples who settled in Ireland preserved a version of the language known as Q-Celtic, while this consonant became modified in Britain and Gaul into a form that is called P-Celtic. The distinction can be illustrated by the present Welsh word for Son, which is Ap, compared to the Gaelic Mac.

Over the greater part of Europe Celtic settlements consisted of villages, as a rule, packed with rectangular houses of timber and thatch. In the British Isles, by contrast, folk were more inclined to settle on individual farms or crofts, and to erect circular houses that were widely scattered about the area of settlement. Such differences in life-style developed between the continental Celts and those who emigrated to the British Isles, while many common traditions continued to attest their cultural kinship. The Celtic immigration into these islands was not a rapid event causing an abrupt transition from bronze to iron using and widespread disruption. In fact the reverse may have been true for there are traces of evidence that the political and kin-ship ties—and even the tribal territories—that were familiar to Caesar five decades before the birth of Christ were not created by iron-age immigrants, but had already existed throughout a great part of the Bronze Age.

Our knowledge of the Celtic peoples of the Iron Age does not rest only upon the dis-coveries of archaeology. It is illuminated also by the comments of classical Greek and Roman writers. Naturally these vary in time and place, like the evidence of material objects dug out of the ground, and throw a brighter light on the continental Celts than on the inhabitants of Britain. In so far as they are applicable to the folk of the Highlands and Islands, this could only be through the affinities between these people and the ones those classical authors were describing. While the experts continue to differ in a field so wide open to speculation, we may enjoy the earliest written remarks which may be applicable to our

The three great Hallstatt periods from the twelfth to seventh centuries B.C. were succeeded by a second great Celtic culture, La Tène, which can be distinguished in Rhineland areas from about 450 B.C. By the following century it had spread to Britain and early in the third century B.C. Celtic migration had reached as far east as Galatia.

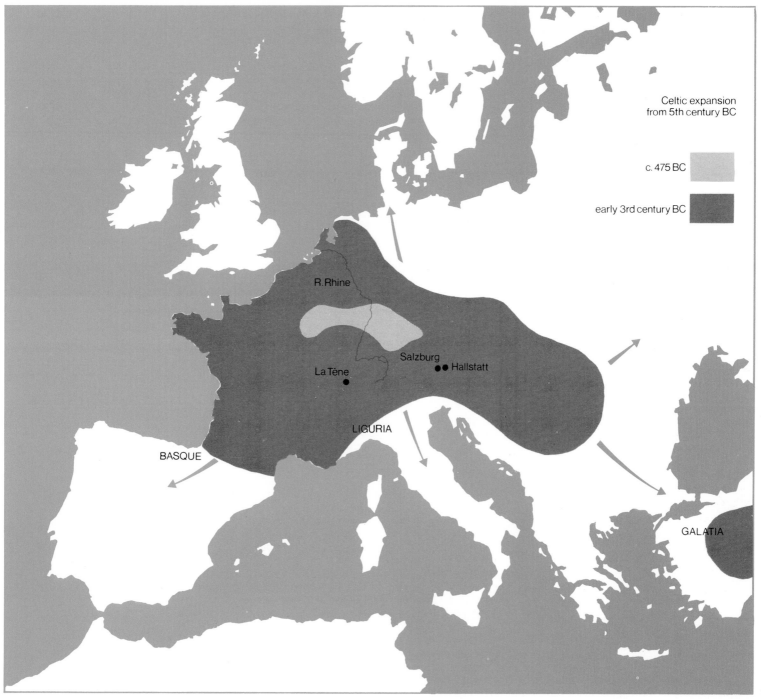

Celtic expansion
from 5th century BC

c. 475 BC

early 3rd century BC

R. Rhine

Salzburg

Hallstatt

La Tène

LIGURIA

BASQUE

GALATIA

41

ancestors, undeterred by questions to which specialists can give no agreed answer.

The classical authors depicted a stratified society dominated by a warrior aristocracy, its economy based largely on cultivation, its top people delighting in lavish ornament. Where the land was less suitable for cultivation, particularly in the Highlands and Islands, flocks and herds were to a greater extent or almost entirely the basis of wealth. But everywhere the Celtic peoples enjoyed fighting, either with an external enemy or among themselves.

The prizes of war were not only gold ornaments and animals, but also human beings. A Greek author mentioned some time before the birth of Christ that the Celts would barter a slave for a jar of wine, a servant for a drink, as though slaves were too easily captured in battle or rounded up in a raid to have a high value, while those of the lowest orders were two-a-penny. Slave chains used for fastening victims in batches with iron collars round their necks have been discovered in Britain, though not in Scotland, so enslavement was practised by the Celts at least in parts of these islands.

As in the Greek and Roman civilisations, there is relatively little evidence of the condition of the lower orders, slave or free. It is the aristocracy whose appearance and life-style are preserved so vividly. To the darker Mediterranean races they presented a splendid appearance, with their fine physiques and fair hair. Strabo the Greek remarked that the young Celts who did not keep themselves fit were fined, and he described the attention they paid to their coiffure. 'Their hair is not only naturally blond, but they also use artificial means to increase this natural quality of colour. For they continually wash their hair with lime-wash and draw it back from the forehead to the crown and to the nape of the neck, with the result that their appearance resembles that of satyrs or of pans.' They shaved their beards but allowed their moustaches to grow.

The male cultivation of his appearance, comparable to that of the Greeks, culminated in the spectacle of the Gaesatae. These were warrior bands that operated outside the tribal framework, a military elite in which we glimpse the possible origins of Finn Mac Cumhaill and his company, the Ossianic heroes of Gaelic legend. 'The Gaesatae had discarded their garments owing to their proud confidence in themselves, and stood naked with nothing but their arms in front of the whole army,' wrote the Greek historian Polybius, describing the battle of Telamon in 225 B.C. and the ritual nakedness of the warring Celt. They wore only their elaborate hairstyles, a mass of gold jewellery, and occasionally a sword-belt round their waists. 'Very terrifying were the appearance and gestures of the naked warriors in front, all in the prime of life and finely built men, and all in the leading companies richly adorned with gold torques and armlets. The sight of them indeed dismayed the Romans, but at the same time the prospect of winning such spoils made them twice as keen for the fight.' The Romans won.

The Celtic women, according to a Greek witness, 'not only equal their husbands in stature, but they rival them in strength as well.' A Roman writer went even further in the course of some trenchant remarks on the quarrelsome nature of the Celt. 'A whole band of foreigners will be unable to cope with one of them in a fight, if he calls in his wife, stronger than he by·far and with flashing eyes; least of all when she swells her neck and gnashes her teeth, and poising her huge white arms, begins to reign blows mingled with kicks like shots discharged by the twisted cords of a catapult.'

Here is no docile Greek consort in a male dominated society, but one of the race of Boudicca, Queen of the Iceni, who led a revolt against the Romans in Britain and whom Dio Cassius described as 'huge of frame and terrifying of aspect. A great mass of red hair fell to her knees.' No wonder the great pre-Christian Gaelic epic called the Táin Bó Cúalnge—the Cattle-raid of Cooley—is dominated by the awesome Queen Medb of Connacht, or that Celtic tribes were named after an ancestral goddess. This was a society in which men had reason to keep themselves agile and presentable in a domestic world that was agressively matriarchal.

The popular penannular neck rings are called torcs (or torques) because many, though by no means all, are made of spirally twisted gold or bronze. A detail of a bracelet (left) from Waldalgesheim in the German Rhineland, has a decoration into which human faces have been worked.

43

How did such a race of men and women, which had dominated Europe and terrorised Greece and Rome, decline until it found its last foothold on the very rim of western Europe? Perhaps the answer is quite simply that they stopped fighting and became civilised. An innate lack of disciplined organisation was a contributory cause then, as it was to remain over a thousand years later. In war, Polybius noticed it at the critical battle of Telamon where the Gaesatae 'rushed wildly on the enemy and sacrificed their lives, while others retreating step by step on the ranks of their comrades, threw them into disorder by their display of faint-heartedness.' Again and again they showed themselves as easily demoralised by failure as they were elated by success.

They embarked on strife almost frivolously and without method. 'The whole race which is now called Celtic or Galatic,' wrote Strabo, 'is madly fond of war, high spirited and quick to battle, but otherwise straight-forward and not of devious character. And so, when they are stirred up, they assemble in their bands for battle quite openly and without fore-thought; so that they are easily handled by those who desire to outwit them.' Caesar found them rent by internal dissensions when he set out to conquer Gaul, and it was the same in Britain. Here perhaps, is the prime paradox of the Celts; a long and disastrous failure to achieve political cohesion either in peace or war and a remarkable, widespread cultural unity.

The lives of the Celts were surrounded by rituals and beliefs in which the lower orders probably shared, even if they did not share the gold torques, the glory of death in battle, and the material luxury in which the aristocracy revelled, and which they sought to take with them beyond the grave. The innumerable Celtic gods and goddesses were in many cases divine ancestors like those of the Greeks and Romans. Just as Celtic women were often more than equals of the men, so were the goddesses at least the equals of the gods. One of the most powerful of the female divinities was Macha the horse goddess, not surprisingly since the rise of the Celts owed an incalculable debt to their mastery of this animal. Another

animal of the utmost significance to the Celts was the boar. Superb bronze effigies have been found in Europe, the bristles along the spine accentuated in the manner affected by the Celtic warriors in their hair-styles. The boar personified courage and strength and an example of the Celtic pantheon was a god called Moccus, meaning Pig, the name of the island of Muck in the Hebrides.

The priesthood of Gaul and Britain in the first century B.C. ranked high in the nobility and priestly authority was extensive since religion pervaded every activity. It was the priests who organised and led the resistance to the Romans and Latin records of them are usually hostile and one-sided. Caesar, how-ever, wrote of them in Europe: 'The Druids are concerned with the worship of the gods, look after public and private sacrifice and expound religious matters; a large number of young men flock to them for training, and hold them in high honour.' They imparted their learning, not through the medium of writing, but by memory training and, if

Caesar is to be believed, 'they have the right to decide nearly all private and public dis-putes, and they also pass judgement and decide rewards and penalties in criminal and murder cases, and in disputes regarding legacies and boundaries.' Caesar was con-vinced that the druidic religion originated in Britain and remarked that anyone who wished to study it should go to Britain to do so. Writing a few decades later, Pliny suggested that the druids maintained their religion at a high pitch of enthusiasm in these islands. 'At the present day Britain is still fascinated by magic, and performs rites as though it was she who had imparted the cult to the Persians.'

Tacitus, son-in-law of Agricola, recorded the frightful scenes when the druid sanctuary on Anglesey was stormed in A.D. 59, the women once again playing an important part: 'On the shore stood the opposing army with its dense array of armed warriors, while between the ranks dashed women in black attire like the furies, with their hair dishevelled, waving brands. All round the druids, lifting up their

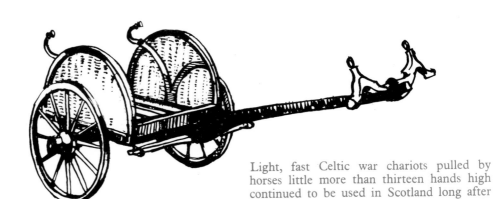

Light, fast Celtic war chariots pulled by horses little more than thirteen hands high continued to be used in Scotland long after their form of warfare had died out first in Gaul then in southern Britain. The horse was an animal of high cult importance but the boar and stag had a greater pre-eminence in pagan Celtic mythology.

hands to heaven and pouring forth dreadful imprecations, scared our soldiers by the unfamiliar sight so that, as if their limbs were paralysed, they stood motionless and exposed to wounds. Then, urged by their general's appeal and mutual encouragements not to quail before a troop of frenzied women, the Romans bore the standard onwards, smote down all resistance, and wrapped the foe in the flames of his own brands. A force was set over the conquered, and the sacred groves, devoted to inhuman superstitions, were destroyed.'

This was an exceptionally important druid centre, from which it cannot be doubted that many priests succeeded in escaping to Ireland and possibly to Scotland though no sanctuary of equal significance has been identified in the Highlands: the notion that the druids were associated with such monuments as Stonehenge or Callanish is the invention of a much later age when this ancient priesthood of a barbaric society recaptured the imagination of many and sparked off all kinds of romantic speculations.

The arts of the Celts were to enjoy a spectacular future. Developed originally on the continent they had, by the third century B.C., reached a peak of invention that still astonishes. The skills of the smiths, masons and carvers, ministered to the Celtic passion for display, the exuberance of the Celtic religion, producing horse-harness and jewellery, domestic utensils and the human figures and heads with great staring eyes, intricate convolutions of design, geometrical and naturalistic, abstract patterns into which faces were woven with a subtlety that has been described as the most graphic surviving expression of the tortuous and complex Celtic character. Its patrons had already brought it to the British Isles by the time it reached its zenith on the continent. By 100 B.C. it had declined there, and Roman colonisation completed the damage, substituting for it the products of provincial mediocrity.

Beyond the Roman influence the extraordinary vitality of the Celtic tradition also waned temporarily but it burst out afresh in the incomparable achievements of the gospel illuminations of Iona, the high stone crosses and the sculpture of the Picts which filled the land from Argyll to Shetland.

The Iron Age inhabitants of the Highlands and Islands used a house-style well known in parts of Europe where Strabo describes one of the homes as 'large and circular, built of planks and wickerwork, the roof being of thatch'. Over five hundred years before he wrote these words, the pre-Celtic folk of Shetland, as we have seen, had built themselves a little group of similar houses in stone at Jarlshof, possibly the prototype of the wheelhouse that the native settlers were to build throughout the region. Elsewhere, where there were ample supplies of timber, the round houses could be made of wood in the manner described by Strabo. The most distinctive of these, requiring a veritable forest of trees to be felled by axe, were the crannogs that stood on wooden platforms or artificial islands in lochs. Unlike the Jarlshof houses these were solitary dwellings and they evidently required protection either from human enemies or from wild animals. The remains of some of them have been found with evidence of burning, whether by accident or by hostile action, and of re-occupation. The dates of these homes are uncertain and they are the exception rather than the rule, though they do help to illustrate the longevity of Celtic tradition. Six hundred years after they had been adopted in central Europe a Roman author noted in the third century A.D. the practice of the Caledonians some of whom 'dwelt in bogs', and over a thousand years later still, a crannog was built in the waters off Fort William.

Immigrants who took the western sea-routes to settle in the outer Hebrides built more sophisticated round houses than those of Jarlshof and amongst those that have been excavated the Late Iron Age one at Kilpheder in South Uist is typical. It is a little over eight metres in diameter, by no means the largest of its kind, and besides its entrance it possesses a passage leading directly to a neighbouring home. The recesses were formed by overlapping stones into little, roofed beehive cells or apses, a refinement that contrasts with others like the wheelhouses on North

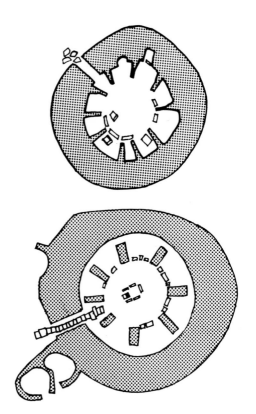

The interiors of wheelhouses are divided by radial, stone piers which supported a timber and turf roof. In those known as aisled wheelhouses the piers are freestanding being joined to the walls only by a lintel. Some houses, like the one at Clettravel, N. Uist, stood in a farmyard enclosure which contained work areas, byres and barns; at Jarlshof the first wheelhouse was built in the yard of the broch, at Clickhimin, Shetland, into the broch itself.

Interior of a wheelhouse, Jarlshof, Shetland. The roof of the first wheelhouse here was supported on timber posts later replaced by freestanding stone piers. The house was eventually dismantled and replaced by two superbly built wheelhouses with radial piers corbelled at the top to roof individual bays.

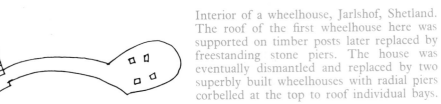

At an early stage of this rebuilding a souterrain was constructed beneath the courtyard of one of the houses. Scottish souterrains, underground drystone structures usually have long, often curving, passages leading to lintelled, not corbelled, chambers which form an early kind of cold store.

Ronaldsay in Orkney, whose 'wheel-spokes' could never have supported a roof in this way.

We can picture the settlers establishing homes like those of Kilpheder in the machair lands along the Atlantic coast at a time when they were as fertile as they are now. They were iron-using folk who could spin and weave woollen cloth both for clothing and to provide privacy for themselves by placing hangings over the entrance to their separate recesses. They fished from curraghs, hunted with slings and iron-tipped spears (for they were great meat eaters), cut peat for fuel, plied their bobbins and spindle whorls, carded with combs of bone and horn. Souvenirs of the outstanding metalwork of their continental forebears took the form of inlaid brooches and, as they drew friezes of animals round their pots, they were forging the rather slender artistic links between past and future.

What did they look like? Since their culture was distinctly Celtic, one might suppose that they possessed the appearance described so consistently by Greek and Roman authors over a period of centuries, with fair hair and womenfolk as large as their men. So why do Hebrideans today not possess the physical characteristics of the warrior aristocracy whose deeds they were to relate for centuries to come in their Ossianic legends, especially since the next infusion of blood was to be that of the tall, fair-haired Vikings.

A legend has spread throughout an enormous area from the Faroe Islands to County Kerry in Ireland, wherever people who are supposed to be tall and fair are found instead to be thick-set and dark. It explains that after the defeat of the Armada in 1588 a few Spanish sailors wrecked on various western coasts were given the role of stud bulls instead of being slaughtered, and such was their virility, and such was the complaisance of the women and their husbands, that the stock was entirely altered to its present appearance. It is noteworthy that wherever this myth is purveyed, it is apt to be reinforced with tales of intermarriage with seals. Early in the nineteenth century a Minister's daughter on the north coast of Scotland offered serious confirmation of the seal story, while the Hewisons of Westray in Orkney explain why they are known as the Dons with unassailable conviction to this day.

Some students of pre-history suggest a more convincing explanation. At the time when the Celtic invaders swept through Europe, it was inhabited by non Indo-European peoples who were defeated, enslaved or pushed into inaccessible regions. Amongst these were the Ligurians who became concentrated in the Italian Alps and in Corsica, where Seneca remarked in A.D. 41 that they still spoke their Ligurian tongue. Others were the Basques who speak their own non Indo-European tongue in the Pyrenees to this day. In Caesar's time they still occupied a significant part of Gaul with their own laws and customs, despite the double menace of the Celts and Romans. But by then a great number of these dark, aboriginal inhabitants had lost their language and traditions; those who had not were the ones who had settled in remote places.

Today, so long do genetic characteristics persist, there is still a similarity between the blood groups of the Ligurian lands, the Basque country, Wales, Ireland and the Scottish Highlands, which cannot be explained as accidental and it is this which accounts for the similarity in racial appearance. The native of that bastion of Gaelic culture, the Isle of Scalpay, Harris, who was mistaken for an Egyptian during the Second World War, with his black hair, dark skin and eyes and short, powerful frame, might well be descended from the megalith builders of the islands. But it is at least likely that his forebears were later European emigrants who did not care to belong to the bottom rung of the Celtic hierarchy.

Strife, as we have seen, was not however limited to continental Europe. Fortifications of increasing architectural sophistication continued to dominate the landscape of the Highlands and Islands and some two to three hundred years after the construction of the vitrified fort of Dun Lagaigh mentioned earlier another type begins to appear in the western isles and Argyll. Known by the Gaelic name, Dun, these numerous, relatively small dry-stone forts have a round or D-

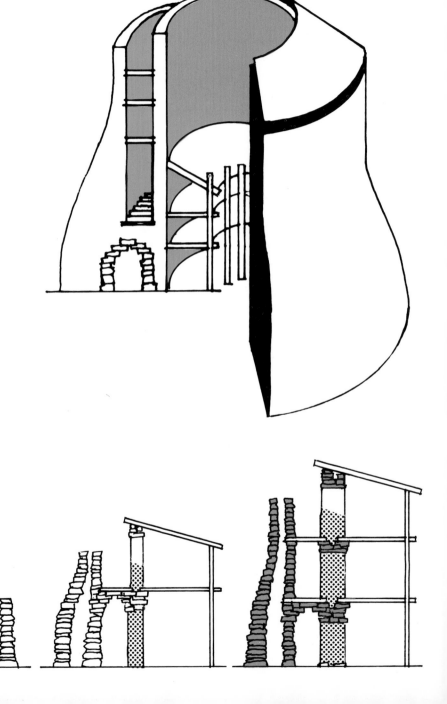

The earliest known Scottish forts, built at a time when bronze was the main metal in use, have a stabilised lacing of timbers in their rubble filled walls. Timber baulks which faced the ramparts in some areas were replaced in the Highlands and Islands by drystone walls through which 'the horizontal timbers sometimes protruded. With wooden ranges built onto the inner wallface, these structures were susceptible to fire caused either accidentally or by enemy action. Sixty or so examples are known in Scotland in which the heat generated by such fires fused or vitrified a part of the stone and rubble infill.

The brochs of the first century B.C. to the second century A.D. represent a peak of achievement. Elaborate and superbly effective defences with ingenious light dry-stone hollow walls which allowed them to be built to literally towering heights, they have no counterpart outside Scotland and, for the most part, not outside the Highlands and Islands. Archaeologists have traced their development from the small fortified sites, the western duns, and galleried duns of Skye and its 48 adjacent areas.

shaped plan. Since their uncomplicated architecture continued to be used over a long period, and few of them have been examined scientifically, it is difficult to say more about them other than that they confirm the general pattern of settlement in north and west Scotland during the late first millennium B.C. and the early first millennium. In the main it was different from that found elsewhere, being of small units based on fortified homesteads though there are less obviously defensive types of settlements, c.490–175 B.C., such as the hundreds of hut circles scattered about the moors of Sutherland.

In Skye a more impressive fortification, the great round stone tower of the broch, is found. Other examples survive at Glenelg on the mainland opposite, and there is a particularly magnificent one at Carloway in Lewis, but by far the greater number were built in Caithness, Sutherland and the northern isles. The broch is a peculiarly Scottish phenomenon which many think evolved on Skye in the first century B.C. The hollow wall of the 'cooling-tower'-shaped broch, sometimes over twelve metres high, had no external apertures except its tiny well-protected entrance. A staircase circulated within the wall to the summit, with openings looking into its round interior. Neither flaming brands nor scaling ladders could achieve a rapid capture of such a structure, and rather than settle to a long seige, a raiding party would have been well advised to go off in search of a more defenceless community. None of the brochs that have been excavated has been found to contain weapons, as one might have expected if they had been the seats of military overlords, and they generally stand close to the shore with a view of the sea approaches in the centre of farming areas. A chain of them was built up either bank of the Naver river in Sutherland, where a message could have been signalled from the one that dominates the approach to the river mouth. Another was built just over a mile from Sumburgh Head in Shetland while the most perfectly preserved stands on the little island of Mousa there.

Although a claim has been made for Skye as the place of origin of the brochs, there are

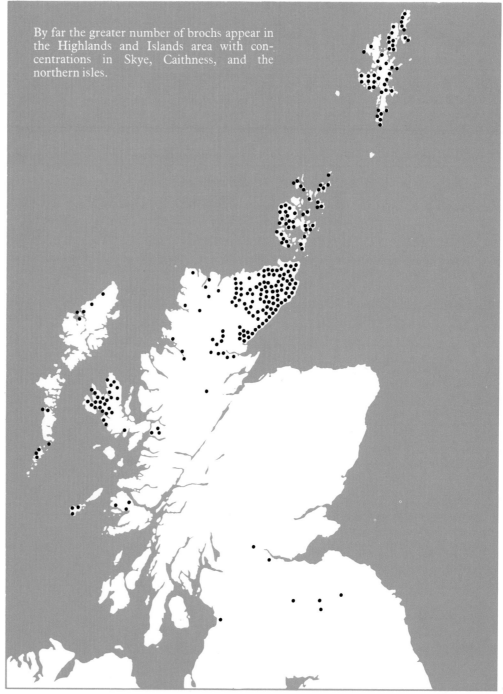

By far the greater number of brochs appear in the Highlands and Islands area with concentrations in Skye, Caithness, and the northern isles.

those who suggest that it was Orkney, that ancient centre of marvellous architectural skill. During the recent excavations at Quanterness, Professor Renfrew's team uncovered a well-built circular structure which they thought at first to be the forecourt of the neolithic tomb. Further examination revealed it to be the remains of a round house, seven and a half metres in diameter, erected in about 800 B.C. Since it appeared to have remained in use until after 200 B.C., the period immediately prior to that assigned to the brochs, it possibly lends some support to the theory of a local evolution of those remarkable fortifications. These fertile islands had not lost their aboriginal inhabitants, but they had been joined by a Celtic aristocracy by the time these sent representatives to the Emperor Claudius seeking to become a client kingdom by formal submission, and thus enjoy the protection of the pax Romana. For it is unlikely that the descendants of local fishermen and farmers would have understood such a procedure, even if their ancestors had helped to build Maes Howe.

'Fortune can give no greater boon than discord among our foes,' wrote Tacitus, and none had abetted fortune more consistently than the Celts. While the chief in Orkney invited Roman protection and fortified his people against their southern neighbours, these maintained an implacable hostility to Roman colonisation. Forty years after the Orcadian plea to Rome, Agricola, governor of Britain from A.D. 78 to 84, brought an army into the Highlands and defeated a Celtic host under Calgacus, which means Swordsman. It is the earliest personal name recorded in Scottish history, and its owner had succeeded in enlisting a formidable coalition of warriors, 30,000 men according to Tacitus. After its defeat a Roman fleet sailed to Orkney and received the submission which had been offered so long before.

The account of these events written by Tacitus includes the oration that Calgacus delivered to his troops before the battle, although the historian could not have heard it, nor have understood it if he had. But he possessed the Roman's knowledge of Celtic eloquence, of Cú Chulainn's gift of speech: and the resounding classical phrases (with their famous taunt, 'where they make a wilderness they call it peace') do not sound out of place in the mouth of a man who probably divided his time between slave-raiding and cattle-plundering. Nor can we assume that the broch and dun builders were any less fond of these sports, or slow to retaliate. But the fact is that, although they were living on the very threshold of recorded history in these islands, the picture of what was going on in the Highlands and Islands at the very beginning of the Christian era remains confused.

This is partly because the victory at Mons Graupius achieved no lasting result there, and the region remained outside the sphere of Roman administration. The dangers which created the brochs evidently receded until many were dismantled to build ordinary homes around their walls and within them. This was done at Sumburgh Head in Shetland as well as in innumerable other places. Midhowe on the Orcadian island of Rousay and Gurness on its mainland both present untidy spectacles of makeshift conversion. Gurness also preserved a grisly reminder of the past, a pair of severed hands flung into the midden before anyone had even removed the five rings from their fingers. They belonged to the superb Celtic tradition of continental metalwork of an earlier age and one may picture their wearer, perhaps tall, blond-haired and bedecked with gold torque and armbands, done to death in one of his raiding expeditions by the broch builders.

The influence of the Roman presence on the Celtic peoples of the British Isles varied greatly. Those who lived within the empire were introduced to urban life, a coinage, roads and regulated trade. Even in the Scottish Highlands beyond people experienced Roman military methods and their own warlike activities must have been affected by these. There were also the trading links, and these were expanded from the 3rd century onwards by a change in the Roman policy of recruitment. To an increasing extent native tribesmen were enlisted to man the frontier forts and garrisons, and settlements consequently grew up around them in which women brought up their children within the culture of the native language and religion although their husbands were in Roman pay. The frontier was maintained as an iron curtain, yet its structure contained as it were a bridge over which passed much traffic.

Agricola had attempted to cast the Roman lassoo round the entire Highland region when he took his army to Mons Graupius, but his victory there was not consolidated. For a time the boundary was established along the Antonine Wall between the Clyde and the Forth, but finally it was withdrawn to Hadrian's wall south of the Cheviots and security in the lands between became increasingly the responsibility of Celtic tribes that evolved into client kingdoms under Roman patronage. The Germanic peoples called such tribes of Romanised Britons 'Welsh', a term that is still applied to their descendants today; and although these dwelt to the south of the Highlands, such names as Carmichael and Galbraith commemorate the British infiltration into that world. In the 3rd century Roman authors began to identify the mixed race of Celtic and aboriginal folk who inhabited the uncolonised lands to the north as 'Picts', while they designated as 'Scots' the unconquered peoples of Ireland. Thus the Celts who had settled in these islands over a period of so many centuries became polarised at last into three principal groupings by the events of history.

By the time this occurred they were also separated by the three different forms of the Celtic language they spoke. That of the Picts, which had been introduced as early as the 7th century B.C. by the timber-laced fort builders, was the most archaic form of it and had also become adulterated by the pre-Celtic speech of the region. Welsh was so different from the Gaelic of the Scots of Ireland that St Patrick the Briton spoke in the 5th century of having changed his mother tongue in order to carry out his mission there, and in the 6th century St Columba the Gael needed an interpreter to converse with Picts in Skye.

Such obstacles to communication have always been a fruitful source of discord, and this was increased by the responsibility that the Romanised Britons had undertaken to defend the imperial frontier against Picts and Scots. In 367 these entered into an alliance to invade Britain, and their immediate victims were naturally Celtic garrison troops, their families in the nearby cantonments, and all the other Celtic folk living within the Roman peace. Many of the frontier soldiers deserted to the ranks of the invaders, lured by the promise of booty; others melted for safety into the civilian population. The marauders were repulsed only after much destruction, and then there was a back-lash in the Highlands, whither bands of men who lived by warfare and plunder retired for safety. It was in such conditions as these that the Ossianic legends were born, about a century after the supposed date of death of Finn Mac Cumhaill, the father of Ossian.

Around the time of that invasion of 367 St Jerome, the translator of the Latin Vulgate version of the Bible, was staying in Gaul and noted the behaviour of raiders there who must have sailed either from Ireland or from western Scotland. He observed that they ate human flesh, not as a ritual (it appears) but because they found certain portions of it succulent. Even if there were many communities living their peaceful, unrecorded lives throughout the Highlands and Islands—weaving, fishing, tending their cattle, drawing pictures in the wet clay of their pots and performing their religious ritual—the crime record, during the century in which the first Celtic saints appeared in the land, does not appear to have been less sensational than it is today.

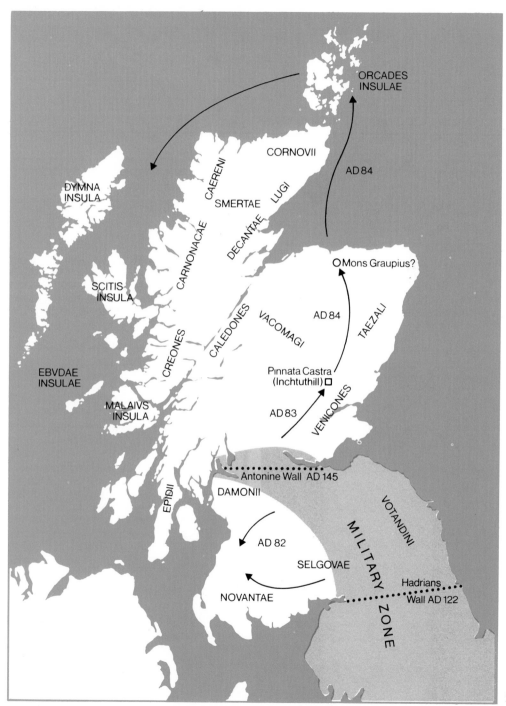

ORCADES
INSULAE

CORNOVII

AD 84

DYMNA
INSULA

CAERENI

SMERTAE

LUGI

DECANTAE

CARNONACAE

Mons Graupius?

SCITIS
INSULA

CALEDONES

VACOMAGI

AD 84

TAEZALI

CREONES

EBVDAE
INSULAE

Pinnata Castra
(Inchtuthill)

MALAIVS
INSULA

AD 83

VENICONES

Antonine Wall AD 145

EPIDII

DAMONII

VOTANDINI

AD 82

MILITARY ZONE

SELGOVAE

Hadrians
Wall AD 122

NOVANTAE

53

Christianity had been established as the official religion of the empire before the death of Constantine in 337. About a century later, after the last of the legions had left Britain, a church leader of British stock named Ninian was selected in the kingdom of Strathclyde, having studied in Rome. Although so little is known for certain about his life, it may be assumed that he did conduct a Christian mission to the Picts. But it is doubtful whether he penetrated far, if at all, into the Highlands or achieved much lasting success among the Picts, though a later cult of St Ninian led to dedications as far north as Shetland.

During St Ninian's lifetime there grew up another Romanised Briton called Patrick, and his is the earliest native voice preserved in his own writings. They tell the dismal story of raids between the Welsh, Picts and Scots, in one of which he was carried off to Ireland. Patrick 'had for my father Calpornius a deacon, the son of Potitus a presbyter, who belonged to the village of Bannavam Taberniae, for near it he had a small villa, where I was made a captive. I was then sixteen years old.' He wrote this in the Latin of the defunct Roman administration, now given a new lease of life by the Christian church.

He admitted that he had not been taught Latin thoroughly, and when he began his missionary activities in Ireland he was handicapped also by the need to exchange Welsh for Gaelic. 'I feared lest I should transgress against the human tongue, seeing that I am not learned like others who have imbibed both laws and sacred letters in equal perfection by the best means, and who from their childhood never changed their mother tongue.' But Patrick's mission prospered exceedingly, and it was the Church he founded there which presently introduced a new civilisation into the Highlands, based on the Latin and Gaelic languages that had yet to be well established there.

In about 450 Patrick wrote to Coroticus, ruler of the Britons of Strathclyde, reproving him for permitting the traffic in slaves. 'The custom of the Roman Gauls is this. They send holy and fit men to the Franks and other heathens with many thousands of solidi to redeem baptised captives. You slay as many and sell them to a foreign nation that does not know God.' Patrick had been carried off by Irish Gaels: he accused his Welsh countrymen of the same practices: they were, he said, no better than 'the most unworthy, most evil and apostate Picts.' In fact everyone engaged in this lucrative trade that William Wilberforce was still fighting against in the 19th century, and Patrick's words bring home to us the magnitude of the task his Church had shouldered. 'May God inspire them to amend their lives,' wrote the saint, 'and liberate the baptised women captives whom they have taken, so that they may deserve to live to God and be made whole, here and in eternity.'

The way was paved for the dissemination of Patrick's message in the Highlands by the settlement of Scots from northern Ireland in the lands of Argyll. This had taken the form of sporadic infiltration for a long time before Fergus the Son of Erc, under pressure from the powerful house of O'Neill, moved the seat of his little principality of Dalriada across the water from Ulster in about 500. The kindreds of Dalriada believed themselves, indeed, to belong to the stock which had entered eastern Scotland over a thousand years earlier with their timber-laced forts. But although these gave them a remote kinship with the Pictish aristocracy and would help to explain the hostility of the Gaelic O'Neills, the Dalriada folk had become fully absorbed into the Gaelic culture of Ireland and brought it with them to Scotland, where it has flourished ever since.

The immediate advantage of this from a modern viewpoint is that they had entered the light of Gaelic record, in which they can be seen more clearly than either the Picts or the Britons, whose records have not survived so fortunately. They stand revealed as a Celtic warrior aristocracy in the antique mould, and one organised to conduct maritime as well as land operations, every twenty houses being obliged to provide two seven-benched boats. Their expansion into Argyll was part of a widespread thrust overseas which planted Gaelic-speaking settlers in Galloway, in the isle of Man and in Wales. But the northern colony was to prove the most enduring. Centres were established in Islay, at Dunollie overlooking the

Almost by force of circumstance the Picts were a warlike people. About A.D. 500 Fergus Mor, son of Eric, moved the seat of Dalriada from his palace at Dunseverick, County Antrim, to Dunadd in Argyll. The Scots, however, were not the only threat to the Picts; there were the Britons of Strathclyde and more particularly the Angles, Germanic invaders who gradually extended their kingdom from northeast England as far north as the Firth of Forth and by A.D. 638 were poised to attack Pictland itself.

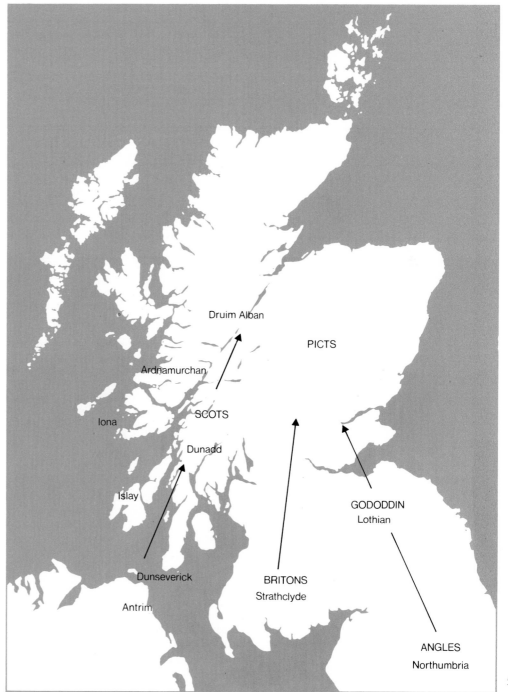

Druim Alban

PICTS

Ardnamurchan

SCOTS

Iona

Dunadd

Islay

GODODDIN
Lothian

Dunseverick

BRITONS
Strathclyde

Antrim

ANGLES
Northumbria

Firth of Lorne and on the rock of Dunadd that rose out of the Crinan bogs; and an uneasy boundary was pushed to Ardnamurchan in the north and the hills of Drium Alban in the west. Dunadd is the best-preserved of the earliest Scottish capitals. Its entrance is a steep path through a natural cleft in the rock, and the fortified terraces above were crowned by solid rock near the summit in which a footprint had been hollowed. Here kings placed one of their feet at the ceremony of inauguration. The stone also possessed a linear carving of a boar that is Pictish work. Perhaps it was chiselled by the Picts when they captured Dunadd: but it might have been commissioned from a Pictish craftsman by the rulers of Dalriada, this ancient symbol that was to be the totem of the Campbells in this very region centuries later.

The office of Righ (King) was a sacred one as it had always been. He was the ruler of a kindred, which consisted of all the descendants of a particular pair of great-grandparents. If the numbers were small, they were nevertheless augmented by the Celtic laws of marriage, which Christianity did not immediately restrain. There were ten permitted forms of union, including marriage to a second wife whose relations with the first were carefully defined, and concubinage. Divorce was allowed by mutual consent.

These arrangements may appear to have been destructive of family life, but they belonged to a society that did not consist of individuals so much as groups of kinsfolk in which the children were in many cases brought up under a system of fosterage. They then received their entire education from their foster-parents, the boys until they were seventeen years old, the girls until fourteen. Their relations remained particularly close throughout life with their foster-brothers and sisters and they were obliged to maintain their foster-parents in old age. So their affections, loyalties and standards of behaviour were governed by a different domestic structure from that of a modern society officially monogamous. Fosterage still survived in the Highlands over a thousand years later.

The Righ, or head of a kinship group, was not necessarily the eldest male heir since it was required that he should be without blemish. This did not extend only to physical deformity: a king might be dethroned if he was found to be untruthful, since these people shared with Hindus the Indo-European belief that the truth possesses a magic of its own, and can destroy those who flout it. The man chosen for the succession was married sacramentally to the goddess who personified sovereignty. Macha the horse goddess fulfilled this role and it has been suggested that Queen Medb was in reality such a being, because the *Táin* epic tells that she was the wife of nine kings, and that only a man who mated with her could obtain regal status. Kindred kings were subject to higher kings, who in turn were junior to provincial monarchs. Royalty was in fact a warrior ruling class, selected on grounds of merit and ritually consecrated.

Beneath it came that of the nobles, who consisted of men of religion and learning as well as warriors; and scarcely beneath them in rank were rated the craftsmen in wood and metal, the men of medicine and of law. With the coming of Christianity the druids lost their functions, while the fili became poets, men of letters and historians, still retaining an ancient status somewhat resembling that of Brahmins in India, and undergoing a twelve year course of training for their office. The third order consisted of the husbandmen, while the nature of the fourth is, as usual, somewhat obscure. There were certainly slaves, although it is thought that these were few in number and generally captives in war. It is not known to what extent the original population were evicted, reduced to serfdom, or simply permitted to continue their farming and their crafts without molestation in the kingdom of Dalriada.

As in their marriage customs, the Scots here conducted their relations with one another through an elaborate code of laws of great antiquity. All disputes, including one involving homicide, were argued before a judge who received a fee for his services, and the details for enforcing justice were laid down in detail. In Hindu law a creditor fasted before the door of his debtor until the latter gave satisfaction, and so it was in Gaelic law. The plaintiff could fast before the defendant's house from sunset until sunrise, and if the defendant did not follow his example he became liable to double his debt in damages.

The Celts in Europe had based their society on a rural way of life until they were conquered, and to a remarkable extent those who had been Romanised in Britain abandoned urban living after the legions were withdrawn. In uncolonised Ireland and Pictland they had never concentrated in towns or villages, although they possessed strongholds and sanctuary sites at which they gathered in assemblies. They used no coin currency, but estimated their wealth in cattle, a preference that survived in the Highlands into the 18th century.

Both men and women wore a long linen shirt, such as the soldiers of Montrose were wearing on that hot summer day in 1645 when they flung aside their plaids and knotted the shirt tails between their legs for decency, to win the battle of Kilsyth. Over the shirt they donned a short tunic and a square woollen cloak fastened with a brooch. Their staple diet was bread and porridge, with beef and pork on festive occasions and beer and mead for their drink. The most popular game was evidently comparable to chess, with two sets of figures on a chequered board. Children enjoyed a ball game known as 'driving the hole.'

Nothing like the same information survives concerning the way of life of the majority of people living in the Highlands and Islands, as of this small minority who had created Dalriada in Argyll. We know that a century or so later these consisted of three kindreds numbering 560, 420 and 430 households. Over five hundred years earlier Calgacus was said by Tacitus to have brought an army of 30,000 men to Mons Graupius, and even if this was an exaggeration it is obvious that the Pictish population was very much larger than the Scottish one, although much of it lived outside the Highlands. But not a single complete sentence of its language survives, its traditions are lost, and its records consist of little more than lists of kings.

But the regime under which it lived had been planted in Scotland for at least as long a time as separates the modern Highlander from the reign of King Macbeth. The Romans had conceded that it possessed formidable military power, which involves organisation as well as a warlike attitude. Its fleets controlled the seas of the northern and western isles, though they could not dominate eastern waters in which the continental fleets operated.

Place-name studies indicate that while the Celtic tongue became corrupted in the south, it may scarcely have been used in the far north at all. The most un-Celtic practice, however, that seems to have prevailed throughout Pictland was the system of matrilinear succession. It would have enabled the original Celtic colonists to marry rather than fight their way into top positions, and whether they did this or not, the King Lists testify that by the beginning of the historical period this law of succession was well established: and when an incoming aristocracy had adopted it, then surely the aboriginal inhabitants could not have abandoned it.

The earliest notable sovereign was Bridei son of Maelcon who reigned in northern Pictland and played his part in some of the most formative events that have occurred in the Highlands. He had already taken the offensive against the Scots of Argyll and defeated them several years before these were joined by a member of the royal Irish house of O'Neill, once known as Colum Cille, the Dove of the Church, and now remembered as St Columba. As the great-grandson of a King he stood in the line of succession, and although he embraced the religious life he anticipated the career of those prince-prelates who were among the most powerful statesmen of a later age. In 563 Columba sailed to Scottish Dalriada to set up his headquarters on Iona, off the island of Mull, and although the Irish annals stated that the donation came from the King of Dalriada, it appears that it was more probably the gift of King Bridei of the northern Picts. And while Iona appears today typical of the remote places in which Celtic monks chose to retire from the world, it then constituted an outpost of the utmost strategic importance on the threshold of the Pictish islands, and with convenient access by sea to the pass of the Great Glen.

The Monymusk Reliquary, a casket made about A.D. 700 to hold the bones of St Columba who is credited with the conversion of the Picts. St Columba was given Iona for his monastery in A.D. 563 by Bridei, son of Maelcon and one of the earliest Pictish kings about whom little other than his name is known. St Columba died on Iona in A.D. 597 at the age of seventy-three; it was not long before he became a saint of real importance whose bones were holy relics.

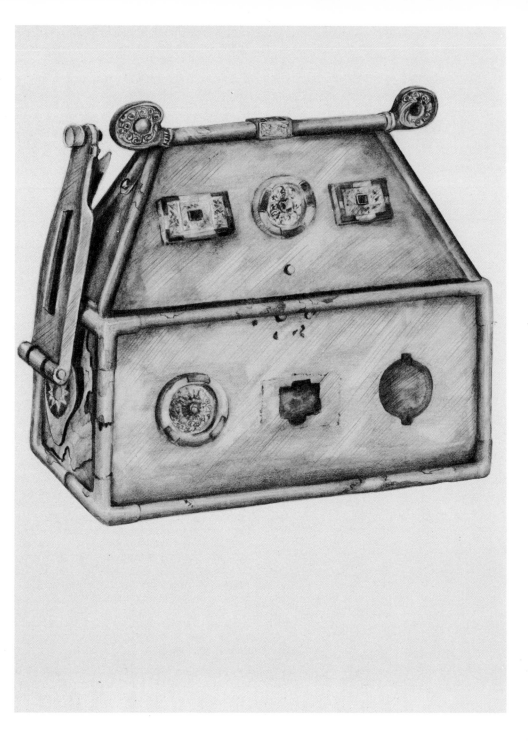

Thither Columba made his famous journey to visit King Bridei at his headquarters in Inverness and caught sight of a monster in Loch Ness on his way. Bridei accepted the Christian message and gave Columba's missionaries safe-conducts to proceed to Orkney, whose under-king was then at the Pictish court. Whether this visit occurred before or after Columba's settlement on Iona is uncertain, but it is significant that the British saint Comgall accompanied Columba on his mission to King Bridei, and that other British missionaries shared in the great task of conversion. Comgall and Moluag planted foundations in Skye, Lismore and Tiree, while Donnan from the island of Eigg may have penetrated to Kildonan in Sutherland which is named after him. Even if this is a later dedication, it recalls an enterprise which united the warring Britons, Picts and Scots in Christian brotherhood.

But it was not exclusively the sword of the spirit that made a Scotland out of Pictland. In 574 Aiden succeeded as King of Dalriada, her outstanding ruler with Columba's active backing. Dunadd was his capital, and from here he led a victorious army into British territory in 578 and a naval expedition through Pictish waters to Orkney in 580, one of his many maritime enterprises. He outlived King Bridei, who died in 584, and seems to have increased Scottish power at the expense of the Picts although the records of their strife are somewhat confused.

Columba died in 597 and barely a century later his life was written by Adomnan, the 9th Abbot of Iona and another member of the kindred of O'Neill. This earliest of Scottish biographies testifies in its elegant Latin and its literary allusions that Iona had already joined the main-stream of the European cultural world, with standard books of reference and well-informed monks. It emphasises Colum the Dove rather than Columba the statesman, particularly in its description of the saint's last hours. 'He climbed a small hill overlooking the monastery, and stood on its summit for a little while. And as he stood, he raised both hands, and blessed his monastery, saying: "on this place, small and mean though it be, not only the Kings of the Irish with their peoples, but also the rulers of barbarous and foreign nations, with their subjects, will bestow great and special honour; also especial reverence will be bestowed by saints even of other churches". After these words he descended from that little hill, returned to the monastery, and sat in the hut, writing a psalter. And when he came to that verse of the 33rd psalm where it is written, "but they that seek the Lord shall not want for anything that is good," he said, "here, at the end of the page I must stop. Let Baithene write what follows." '

One Gaelic elegy is thought to be a genuine composition of the 6th century, and it contains the lament: "No longer there remains to us he who used to keep us from all fears; never shall he come back to us, who used to declare the word of truth; no longer to us he who used to teach the tribes of Tay, and whom the world knew. We are as a harp without string pins, as a church without an abbot." And although a Gaelic poem attributed to Columba himself is in the language of a later century, it enshrines his love of books and an aspect of his character as Adomnan described them. "I send my little dripping pen unceasingly over an assemblage of books of great beauty, to enrich the possessions of men of art—whence my hand is weary with writing." Such was the man who had such a profound formative influence on the Highlands, as men remembered him there.

This influence spread gradually to the remotest communities throughout the glens and islands, bringing the language and the religion that have shaped the thoughts and lives of their descendants to this day. In many cases we can only guess the date of the religious centres that were planted in such places as the Broughs of Deerness and Birsay in Orkney, and little isles such as Eileach an Naoimh and Canna in the Hebrides. Hand in hand with the spiritual teaching came the traditions of those who brought it, binding the remote past to a distant future.

One of the most remarkable illustrations of this is preserved in some ballads that were written down in the Highlands in the 16th century. Unlike the Lowland ballads, which describe comparatively recent events, several of these dramatise that epoch-making confrontation of a thousand years before, when

St Patrick opposed his Christian values to those which had been practised for so long by the pagan Celts. Ossian, son of Finn mac Cumhaill and last survivor of the Fenian company, asks the saint:

"Tell us, Patrick, in honour of your learning, have the nobles of the Fenians of Ireland, in particular, won heaven?

I will tell you truly, Ossian of brave deeds, heaven is not for your father, for Osgar nor for Goll.

It were little pleasure for me to sit in the heavenly city without Caoilte or Osgar or my father beside me.

It is better to see, but for one day, the face of the Son of heaven, than that all the gold in the universe should be in your possession.

For your honour's love, Patrick, do not forsake the men. Without the knowledge of the King of heaven, do you admit the Fenians.

Though small is the buzzing gnat or the mote in the sunbeam, neither could come under the rim of His shield without the knowledge of heaven's King.

It was not so with Cumhaill's son, a noble king among the Fenians. All the world might enter his house without asking.

Aged man, I pity you, and you at your life's end. That is not a just judgment that you give of my King.

Greater the worth of one stout troop that Finn of the Fenians used to bring than yourself and your Lord of piety together."

These are just a few of the exchanges that echo the quandary of the Celtic Church's missionary days. Another of the ballads preserved a conversation between Cú Chulainn's widow and the man who had avenged his death. Like the head-hunters of old, he was carrying his grisly trophies in triumph, and she asked him to identify each in turn, an even earlier theme than those discussed by St Patrick and Ossian.

The Gaelic tradition enshrined also a gift that has been treasured in the Highlands ever since. Kuno Meyer described it as occupying 'a unique position in the literature of the world. To seek out and watch and love Nature, in its tiniest phenomena as in its grandest, was given to no people so early and so fully as to the Celt.' We can only guess how fast and how far this influence was carried into the farthest corners of the region: but it was the saints and hermits of the Celtic church who engendered it, and many of these chose the remotest places for their meditations. The compositions that survive have turned up in countries that recall the range of Celtic missionary activities—for instance the delightful Gaelic verses in a 9th century manuscript in Switzerland.

"A hedge of trees surrounds me, a blackbird's lay makes music for me—I shall tell it. Above my lined book the trilling of the birds makes music."

Mediaeval Scottish Gaelic poetry retained this vision and love of the natural world, which blossomed again in the eloquence of Duncan Bàn Macintyre's songs in the 18th century.

There is no reason to doubt that the Picts possessed comparable traditions, just because they perished with the language or languages in which they were enshrined. Indeed, if the sculptural arts of the Picts are anything to go by, these are likely to have been of outstanding richness and originality. For in a less perishable medium they created what Nora Chadwick has described as 'a richly furnished album in stone, which knows no predecessors, no close affinities'. It survives from Shetland in the north to Fife in the south and as far west as the Hebrides; and the earliest class consists of geometrical symbols and stylised representations of animals and birds incised with a masterly control of line on undressed stone surfaces. These have been dated to a period between 500 and 700. Isabel Henderson has drawn particular attention to the symbol stone at Golspie in Sutherland as an outstanding example in support of her theory that much of the inspiration behind this art originated in the north. Such an interpretation is consistent with the historical fact that Bridei son of Maelcon, whom Saint Columba visited in Inverness, was remembered as the most powerful ruler of his time in Pictland, even though it is impossible to date any particular sculptures with certainty to his reign.

The commonest of all the Pictish symbols supports the theory of a northern influence. It resembles a pair of dividers (generally called a

The stone sculptures of the Picts fall broadly speaking into three main classes. First, pagan symbol stones, 7th century, with fourteen enigmatic symbols always carved in various combinations like the 'swimming elephant' and the 'mirror'. Second, the cross slabs of the 8th century with fanciful animals and figures, horsemen and hunting or Biblical scenes added to the terse symbolism; the Papil stone demonstrates this second class quite clearly with its four clerics below the cross and the two curious bird-men at the bottom.

The third main class is found in the high Christian crosses of the 9th and 10th centuries.

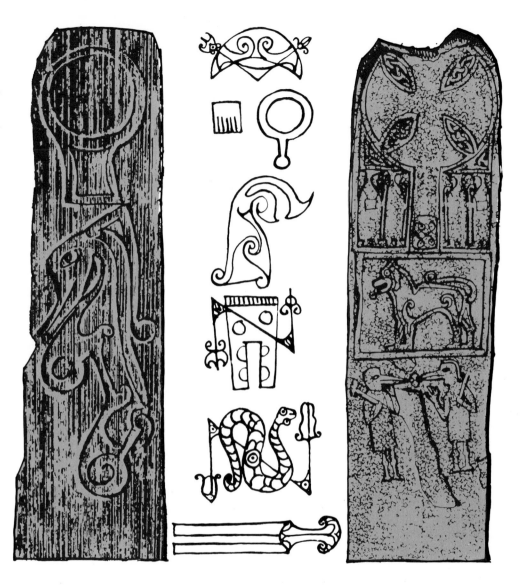

V-shaped rod) laid over a crescent moon, their points decorated with sceptre-like heads, and the crescent also filled with a wide variety of designs. The crescent is found in the Hebrides and Orkney, Aberdeenshire and Fife, but there is a concentration of them in northern Pictland and the example on the Golspie stone has been pronounced a probable prototype of them all.

This stone also contains the most curious and commonest of the animal symbols, a creature sometimes described as a swimming elephant, at others as the Pictish beast. Instead of ears, a long streamer waves from the top of its head along its back: its long snout and mouth have something of the grin of a porpoise: its feet might be built-in roller skates, and its stance suggests a floating forward movement. This beast is found in largest concentration in Aberdeenshire, and in the finest examples (like that of Golspie) combine naturalism with conventional scrolls as brilliantly as the symbolic bulls and boars, stags, birds and horses. The standardisation of these emblems over such a large area suggests a strong cultural unity, and much more besides. For it is generally agreed that they were not merely artistic fancies, but symbols of deep significance; and although their meaning is now lost to us, it was clearly an agreed meaning that was understood throughout the entire Pictish region, representing we know not what degree or form of social cohesion.

The incised symbol stones that predominate in northern Pictland were joined by a second category of sculpture that has been dated to a period between 700 and 900, and that predominates in southern Pictland. The facts of history help to account for this development, which reflects amongst other things the influence of the Angles of Northumbria, and even of the Saxons of the distant south.

The Angles had established a dynasty of rulers with their headquarters at Bamburgh only a few years before Columba came to Scotland. During the ensuing century they expanded north and west until only Strathclyde remained of the British kingdoms in southern Scotland. But their relations with the people of Dalriada beyond took a happier turning when one of their princes fled for refuge to Iona, and returned to become King Oswald of Northumbria in 633. Finding Christianity at a low ebb in his country, he invited Aidan and other monks from Iona to set up a similar monastery on the tidal island of Lindisfarne a short distance to the north of Bamburgh. Oswald himself, the first and (probably) the last English sovereign ever to have made himself proficient in Gaelic, acted as interpreter, as the historian Bede recounted less than a century later.

"The King always listened humbly to Aidan's advice, and diligently set himself to establish and extend the Church of Christ throughout his kingdom. And while the bishop, who was not yet fluent in the English language preached the Gospel, it was most delightful to see the King himself interpreting the Word of God to his thanes and leaders; for he himself had obtained perfect command of the Gaelic tongue during his exile.' In the absence of Pictish comment on the Columban missions, it is all the more interesting to read the comments of Bede the Englishman on the conduct of Aidan. 'The highest recommendation of his teaching to all was that he and his followers lived as they taught. He never sought or cared for worldly possessions, and loved to give away to the poor whatever he received from kings or wealthy folk. Whether in town or country he always travelled on foot, unless compelled by necessity to ride, and whenever he met anyone, whether high or low, he stopped and spoke to them."

In return for the gifts which the Columban church brought to Northumbria, the Highlands received in exchange an invigorating influence that stimulated the arts of the stonemasons, metal-smiths and illuminators of books. It is not always clear beyond dispute, where an inspiration originated, or who was influencing whom. As usual in the story of mankind, these peaceful endeavours of the human heart and mind were not always promoted by a King Bridei or a King Oswald: as often, they were pursued despite the disruptive activities of politicians and generals. One source of discord was the discrepancy between Celtic and Roman church practices—including the dating of Easter—and it reached

Soldier, huntsman and woman, thirsty rider and an unusual figure: carvings show the Picts with long, flowing hair; some men had pointed beards, others moustaches alone. Most people are dressed in long cloaks over ankle length tunics though many of the horsemen wear leggings and one strange character has a short cloak and baggy, pleated shorts. A woman wearing a long full dress and soft cloak is shown riding side-saddle to the hunt; a horseman drinks from a magnificent horn on the tip of which is a decorative bird's head.

a climax in 663. Behind the differences lay the claim of the See of St Peter to supremacy throughout Christendom; and when the King of Northumbria accepted Rome's authority, all the monks who supported their Gaelic bishop left Lindisfarne with him. It was the end of a most fruitful association between Angles and Scots, but not a permanent one. About thirty years later Adomnan, abbot of Iona and biographer of St Columba, adopted the Roman forms, visited Northumbria, and met St Bede who commemorated this encounter between the two great authors. Even at the height of the dispute relations had been dignified, and so they remained.

A few years before the ruling of 663 against the Columban church in Northumbria, the Angles had advanced beyond the Forth and conquered Fife and perhaps considerably more of southern Pictland. They established an Anglian bishopric for this area which lasted until 685 when another King Bridei (in this instance the son of Bili) defeated the Northumbrians at Dunnichen in Angus and recovered the lost territories. After that there was a Celtic revival in southern Pictland, but the influence of nearly thirty years of Anglian church government received only a temporary setback. In about 710 the Pictish King Nechtan adopted the Roman rules and invited the Northumbrians to send architects to help his people build a stone church that he proposed to dedicate to St Peter. The reluctant monks of Iona did not adopt the Roman Easter until 716, and even then there evidently remained a dissenting minority in Pictland whom Nechtan expelled in the following year. Thus the tide of influences ebbed and flowed.

These events are far from the whole story of what was going on during the century after Columba's death. Although the people of the Highlands had moved into the era of written history its records are still thin, and while Gaels and Britons, Picts and Angles contributed to them, those of the Picts are the scantiest of all. This misfortune greatly increases the significance of their rich album in stone, and of the second class of monuments which they fashioned between 700 and 900.

The impact had come from the south, and its creative stimulus was most powerful in southern Pictland. It flooded in from a river that was fed by many tributaries, whose watershed can be observed in some instances, only guessed in others. The metal-work of the Sutton Hoo ship burial discovered in Suffolk and dated to about 625 contains motifs similar to those of the gospel illuminations painted on Lindisfarne between 710 and 720. These in turn possess initial letters resembling those of the inscription on the Ardagh chalice, the great two-handled silver cup which is the glory of early Irish Christian metalwork. Its red and blue enamel band employs a skill that may have come from Persia: while the gospel book of Durrow, illuminated in about 650, contains whole pages of ornamentation that appear to have been derived from Syrian carpets.

The evidence of fabric and woodwork has largely vanished, but stone sculpture has endured to attest its close relationship with the arts of metal and vellum. The freestanding stone crosses were erected at Ruthwell and Bewcastle in Northumbria soon after the Lindisfarne gospels were completed, and a Northumbrian origin has been suggested for the series put up in Ireland during the 8th century. It is against this backbround of cross-fertilisation between different peoples and skills that we must view the Pictish achievement. So far from consisting of mediocre provincial copies of the products of others, it borrowed, with consummate taste, only to create masterpieces of astonishing originality and magnificence.

The Picts did not favour the freestanding cross as it evolved in Northumbria, Ireland and Scottish Dalriada. In many cases they unconsciously adopted the pattern of the sun rising behind the arms of the cross, but they placed this on a rectangular slab cut and dressed for the purpose, on which they were able to create a picture-gallery. They also enlarged the sun so that it reached the end of the cross arms, though more usually they designed crosses without suns, as the Northumbrians and Irish did also. The masterpiece at Nigg churchyard in Ross-shire is of particular interest because its cross is of a design found, not in sculpture, but in the illuminations of the Durrow and Lindisfarne gospels.

One of the best preserved Class II Pictish stones, the sandstone cross slab from Aber-lemno, Angus. On the front a cross in relief decorated with spirals is flanked by inter-twined beasts; the reverse shows Pictish horse and foot soldiers in a battle scene beneath a Z-rod and a triple disc symbol.

For a time the Picts continued their technique of linear drawing by incision in stone at the same time as they adopted the practice of carving in relief, filling the cross itself and the surrounding spaces with intricate interlace, with carved bosses and sometimes with figures as well. But it is on the reverse side of the slabs that these figures contribute to the most illuminating contribution which the Picts made to our knowledge of the so-called Dark Ages. The Aberlemno stone in Angus in particular, which is over seven feet high, portrays a battle scene 'on a scale and of a kind unknown in stone in western Europe at that time'. In saying this, Robert Stevenson, Keeper of the National Museum of Antiquities suggests that it may have been influenced by a wall-painting in France. Another expert, Isabel Henderson, offers the alternative inspiration of embroidery, such as survives only from a later date though it may be presumed to have existed during this period.

The impetus from beyond the Highlands and Islands did not weaken within this region. We have observed the originality of the cross on the Nigg stone. Above it the block has been tapered roughly to the shape of a pediment, on which the hermit saints Paul and Anthony are depicted. Paul kneels beneath the date-palm from which he obtained his food and clothing, while Anthony kneels opposite and between them a raven descends with a loaf of bread in its beak. Beneath crouch two lions conceived, one may assume, by masons who had never set eyes on such creatures yet knew how they had assisted Anthony to bury Paul. The reverse of the stone is sadly damaged, but we can still see its imagery of King David, including a harp and a man with cymbals, according to Psalm 150: 'praise him with stringed instruments and organs. Praise him upon the loud cymbals.' This sculpture, created by a people who have left such scanty written records, is distinguished in its literacy.

Another outstanding monument of Easter Ross is the stone from Hilton of Cadboll. It possesses perhaps the finest of the hunting scenes in stone; a woman rides side-saddle accompanied by two horsemen a trumpeter and dogs; an upper panel of the same size

contains Pictish symbols intricately decorated; and the pair of them are surrounded by a vinescroll frame. This stone is dated to about 800, contemporary with Anglian illumination of the same kind, and it might have appeared to the credulous that an enormous manuscript page had been transformed into stone.

The continuing use of Pictish symbols on stones containing the Christian cross proves that, whatever their significance, it did not conflict with the beliefs of the new religion. In addition to the crescent and V-shaped rod and the pair of roundels on the Hilton stone, larger than the huntsmen below, a much smaller mirror and comb have been carved beside the horsewoman. On the Brough of Birsay, symbols appear in an equally tantalising context. Here the fragments of a stone were found which shows three warriors carrying spears and square shields with four symbols above them, one of them once again the crescent.

There were other noteworthy stones in the northern isles. One of those from Papil in Shetland displays men with the heads and beaks of birds, illustrations of a pre-occupation with monsters that was general throughout Europe at this time and already the subject of books. A later sculpture found at Papil reveals by contrast the influence of Iona, for it depicts a procession of monks and a cowled rider moving towards a free-standing cross such as the Picts did not themselves erect.

Another suggestion of such northern affinities is provided by the similarities between the sculpture of Nigg and the Book of Kells. This supreme masterpiece of gospel illumination is thought to have been made in the decades about 800, and possibly part of the work was carried out on Iona before the manuscript was carried to Kells in Ireland. Iona was first pillaged by Vikings in 795, and in 825 the community there were massacred. When the Book was stolen from the church of Kells in 1006 it was described as 'the great Gospel of Colum Cille . . . the chief relic of the western world.'

Sometimes the sculptors appear to have borrowed their designs from vellum, but in other instances the illuminators may have

The west face of the Kildalton, Islay, non-Pictish or 'Irish type', wheeled high cross, about A.D. 800. The reverse side carries several Biblical scenes and equally elaborate Celtic curvilinear ornament.

copied from stone. A linear representation of an eagle on an Orkney stone which was once thought to have been the model for a similar bird in 8th century gospel fragments now preserved in Cambridge, and there are several other intimations that the artists of the north gave as good as they got in the surge of creative activity which united Angles, Gaels and Picts despite all their conflicts. But the tall free-standing wheel-crosses of the Gael were never adopted by the Picts. In the far north the Celtic cross which stands beside Farr Bay, east of the frontier mountains, is carved on a solid rectangular block although its reverse side is blank, and birds with their necks entwined beneath the foot of the cross are the only natural creatures in the design. It is in the heart of Dalriada that crosses like those in Ireland are to be found, at Kildalton in Islay and on Iona.

Yet the Picts did borrow an alphabet known as Ogam which was probably devised by an Irishman in the 4th century, and in which the earliest surviving writings of his countrymen are preserved. The key to this alphabet is given in *Auraicept na n-Éces*, a Gaelic Handbook of the Learned used by the Filid. It consists of incisions made along a line, as though it had been carved initially along a baton of wood. The vowels were represented by notches on the line, the consonants by different numbers of parallel strokes on either side of it and also across it. The Irish used this writing to commemorate their pagan past, in inscriptions, and when the Picts adopted it in about the 8th century they did something similar. They used this script to preserve in stone the only texts that remain of a pre-Indo-European language that was presumably still in use amongst them. In it are embedded Gaelic words for the cross, and for a son in the sense of a father's son. The latter has been explained as a natural loan-word in a society that may have possessed no word for this relationship since descent in it was matrilinear.

Some names can also be recognised, such as Nechtan. Here is an example from Lunnasting in Shetland of an inscription which ends with this name, an otherwise unintelligible fragment of the language spoken there before Celtic, Norse or English tongues had ever penetrated to these islands.

ettocuhetts ahehhttannn hccvvevv nehhtons

The ogam inscriptions of Pictland are found everywhere in association with the symbols, both preserving equally the mystery of their meaning.

Such are the strands from which the pattern of life in the Highlands and Islands over a thousand years ago must be reconstructed, and they leave much to the imagination.

The people living in the far north and west of Scotland during the 8th century were probably none the worse for their remoteness from the political centres to the south of them. How many of them had learned to understand the Gaelic speech of the Columban church is a matter of surmise. Occasionally they might be visited by monks who could tell of other islands in the ocean to the north-west, Faroe with its storm-swept cliffs and Iceland with its great glaciers and a curdled sea beyond: but these islands were reported to be uninhabited except by a few Celtic anchorites. There were no human contacts to be expected except from the source of every outside influence in their lives, flowing up from the south.

Their prosperity varied with their resources in agriculture, animal husbandry, fish and game. The hoard of beautifully decorated silver buried by a Pictish family in some emergency on the Shetland isle of St Ninian is evidence of considerable wealth: the stone sculpture reveals that specialised crafts were supported by cultured patrons: the introduction of ogam script throughout Pictland during the 8th century attests the literary link through the Columban church with Ireland. Since the largest density of ogam inscriptions in stone have been found in Shetland and they were used to preserve a pre-Celtic language, it may be presumed that a most conservative society lived here, keeping alive their pre-Indo-European institutions together with their ancient speech, without rejecting the Christian civilisation that was now flowering so wonderfully throughout the region.

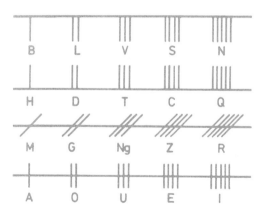

The Ogam alphabet. The Picts spoke two languages, one a form of Celtic, the other, a much older tongue, has been completely lost. Each individual letter of their numerous inscriptions carved in Ogam, an Irish alphabet the Picts most probably learned from the Scots of Dalriada, can be given its English equivalent but with the language lost the words of the inscriptions apart from a few personal names remain undecipherable.

The later and much larger Pictish house was built in Orkney about A.D. 700. From the front an entrance hall leads first into a small room and then into the main living area where on either side of the central hearth wooden benches or beds were raised on stone kerbs. The floor of the last, circular room, most probably a food-store, was paved and its wall corbelled inwards to meet at the top; the remainder of the house was roofed with timber and made waterproof by layers of turf.

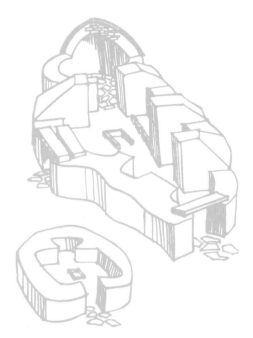

In the northern Hebrides the people may have been relatively poor and backward, afflicted by a deterioration in the weather. The Gaels of Dalriada had settled in strength in the southern Hebrides, and recent research suggests that some of them may have gone as far as Skye to live between the 7th and 9th centuries, and even perhaps to Harris and Lewis. But for the most part these islands contained small communities who have left little evidence to show how strong was the Celtic racial strain or what languages they understood. At the Udal in North Uist archaeology has recently uncovered a most valuable dwelling site, with a long occupation in which we may picture these folk of the 8th century, although we cannot tell with certainty whether their affinities were Irish, Pictish, aboriginal, or in what proportion these were mixed.

Their homes had evolved over a period of five hundred years from single large cells to a complex of cellular houses by the 7th century, and this life-style can be compared with one revealed in a remarkable discovery at Buckquoy, which lies in the fertile lands of Birsay on the north-west mainland of Orkney. Here also there were 7th-century cellular homes, and the final structure consisted of three rooms with an entrance vestibule. Another entrance besides the one passing through this vestibule led by a paved pathway into the main living-hall. The architecture bears some resemblance to that of the homes built around such brochs as Gurness in Orkney and Clickhimmin in Shetland, after these had been abandoned as defensive towers. At the Udal and Buckquoy we have the homes of fairly well-to-do members of a Christian society that was perhaps rather stagnant and self-satisfied at such places on its perimeter. Certainly their inhabitants never dreamt that pagan raiders might suddenly appear out of the empty ocean to the north and east, and the crumbling brochs were of no service to them when the great sails of Viking longships loomed over the horizon.

Their lack of foresight is understandable. Hitherto, for thousands of years, the Highlands and Islands had lain on the outer rim of European activity, and never in recorded history had a human volcano erupted so far north as it now did in Scandinavia. The most outlying Scottish communities were those nearest to the lava-flow, and they were overwhelmed by it.

The eruption began shortly before the year 800 and a rise in population, leading to a search for fresh food supplies, has been given as a principal cause. But in the case of the Swedes it amounted to the expansion of an already flourishing trade, that took them through Russia and across the Black Sea to Byzantium. The Danes assaulted England and the continent to the south of them, while the folk of the Norwegian islands and fjords sailed west until eventually they reached America. The invention of the keel around the year 600 had helped to promote an advance in ship-building and navigational skill, and these were the foundations of the Norse maritime achievement. The emperor Charlemagne's destruction of the Frisian fleets helped to assure Viking command of the seas, and development of the use of sail enabled the Norsemen to make ever longer voyages. But their nearest landfall, Shetland, lay no more than twenty-four to thirty-six hours' sail away, and for half of this time they were not even out of sight of land.

Scandinavia is rich in iron ore, and the outstanding skill of the weapon smiths made its contribution to the Viking conquests. 'Three that are hardest to talk to,' ran an Irish Gaelic saying, 'a king bent on conquest, a Viking in his armour, and a low-born man protected by patronage.' An Irish writer paid tribute to 'the excellence of their polished, ample, treble, heavy, trusty, glittering corslets; and their hard, strong, valiant swords; and their well-riveted long spears.' Their two-edged slashing swords were the pride of this armoury, and the ritual of their manufacture gave rise to legends such as the one that passed into the Wagner's operas of the *Ring* cycle.

Such were some of the motives and techniques that underlay or accompanied the explosive energy of the Viking Age. Undoubtedly the motive of many of the pioneers was simply land-settlement, but what most of western Europe experienced in the first place, and reported with the utmost indignation, was bands of well-armed pagan pirates who dashed ashore to murder and plunder. Their richest targets were undefended centres of religion and learning such as Iona and Lindisfarne where sacred texts, amongst the world's finest master-pieces of book-production, were encased in costly bindings of gold and silver and precious stones. Iona also possessed Scotland's earliest chronicle records, which perished in the holocaust apart from the entries that had been copied into Irish annals: and Isabel Henderson has advanced the suggestion that Maelrubha's foundation at Applecross may have possessed other records which are also lost. For in addition to being pagan, the Vikings were illiterate and therefore placed no value on the written word.

Even where there were no treasures to be found, the raiders could always seize people to carry off into slavery or to hold for ransom, and this became in fact the staple of their commerce. Overnight the Highlands and Islands returned to the conditions against which St Patrick had protested to King Coroticus so many centuries earlier. Such were the rewards of a few days' gangsterism that it was not left entirely to the well-organised syndicates. People who might otherwise have been content to earn their livelihoods by the sweat of their brow were tempted to take it up as a spare-time job during the slack period of the summer.

By this time the Scoto-Irish civilisation was one of the ornaments of Europe, and recognised as such at the court of Charlemagne. Among its luminaries were Sedulius Scotus and John Scotus Eriugena and Dungal who wrote a treatise on the eclipse of the sun, and Dicuil the geographer. It may well have been on Iona that Dicuil recorded his information about the freshwater canal which linked the Nile to the Red Sea until it was blocked up in the year 767, and of the midnight sun that monks had witnessed when they visited Iceland in 795. Dicuil spent many of his latter years in Charlemagne's realm, a part of the brain-drain that was commented upon at the time: 'almost the whole people, despising the dangers of the sea, migrate with their crowd of philosophers to our shores.'

Ireland became a prime objective of Viking enterprise, and it was this that gave an altogether new economic significance to the outlying isles of Shetland, Orkney and the Hebrides, since they were natural springboards for summer raids between seed-time

Starting with raids on the monasteries of Lindisfarne, A.D. 793, and Jarrow, A.D. 794, Viking attacks on Britain rapidly increased; in 851 three hundred and fifty ships entered the mouth of the Thames and their crews stormed Canterbury; by 874 only Wessex under King Alfred held out against the Vikings. The word Viking, meaning pirate, covers all the raiders from Scandinavia. Generally speaking, however, norsemen from Sweden sailed east across the Baltic, the Danes to England and Normandy, and the Norwegians westwards to raid and eventually rule large areas of Scotland, the northern and western isles, the Isle of Man and Ireland.

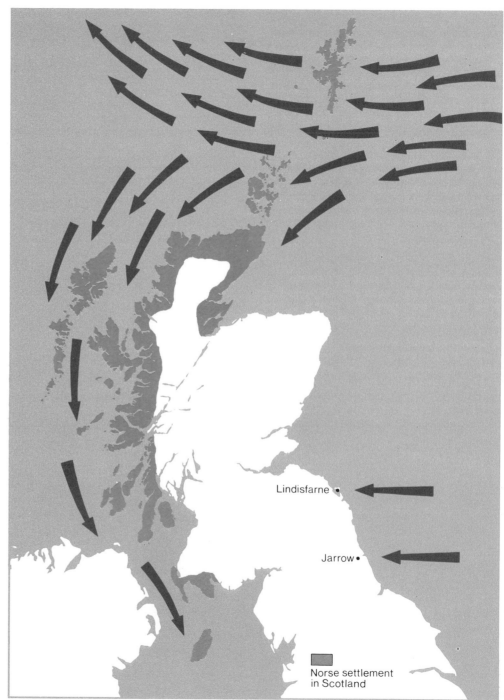

Lindisfarne

Jarrow

Norse settlement in Scotland

and harvest. Between 825 and 850 the rectilinear dwelling of a Norse family replaced the oval architecture of the old inhabitants at the Udal in North Uist, in circumstances that can only be guessed. Equally early, an oblong Norse house was built on top of the Pictish ruins of Buckquoy in Orkney, and a mysterious feature here is that these appear to have been abandoned some time before the new settlers moved in. The archeologists found no evidence of violence in the transition, either because the old inhabitants had been carried off as slaves before the builders of the Norse homestead arrived, or because they had died out or left of their own accord.

In general the picture of the Norse takeover remains blurred, although much valuable evidence has recently come to light and is being augmented yearly by researches such as those of Anna Ritchie at Buckquoy. One of the principal problems to be resolved concerns the testimony of the Christian clerics throughout Europe. 'The destructiveness commonly attributed to the Vikings by annalists and churchmen was much exaggerated.' So runs the argument of an opponent of the romantic view that the Vikings were really awfully decent chaps, defamed by a 'schoolboy myth of barbarous Viking savagery'.

What does emerge from clues that have been uncovered in the region is that Norsemen adopted artifacts of the native people amongst whom they settled to an extent that suggests a close relationship with them. Bone pins found on a number of sites appear to have been made by Picts in a subordinate position for their Norse masters. 'The incomers,' Professor David Wilson has concluded, 'put the local populace to work, ploughing the fields, minding the cattle, weaving cloth and building houses.' Consequently these houses were embellished with the stone-built lateral benches that had been part of the furniture of pre-Norse homes, a feature that was carried across the sea to Scandinavia. In the Norse settlement of Jarlshof on the southern tip of Shetland the loom-weights and spindle-whorls were Norse, whereas stone pounders and possibly slate implements were of native origin. The degree of Pictish servitude remains in doubt.

Wilson comments: 'The indigenous population of a conquered region could no longer afford grand works of jewellery, and had to make do with the poorer materials. But the incomers also adopted some of their fashions.' The northern isles were amongst the first lands to be enveloped in the Viking expansion, and although so few of their homesteads have been excavated there it is evident that the Norsemen settled in great strength since both Orkney and Shetland were transformed into Scandinavian societies, as they have remained ever since. The overwhelming proponderance of Norse place-names in Lewis, and to a lesser extent in North Uist and Skye, suggests that they occupied the northern Hebrides in comparable numbers, and although their language was later eroded by Gaelic throughout the western isles, such names as MacAskill, MacLeod and MacAulay recall the Norse origins of many of their inhabitants.

Had the Viking Age begun even half a century earlier, the outcome might have been different: Gaelic Dalriada might have been altered as permanently as Orkney and Shetland by the Norse presence. For in 729 Oengus fought his way to the throne of Pictland, the most outstanding military leader in the history of that kingdom, and he set out to conquer Dalriada. By 734 his forces had penetrated to Dunollie, the Gaelic stronghold on the Firth of Lorne: two years later Dunadd fell to the Picts: by 741, according to the Irish annalist, Dalriada was overthrown. But Oengus tried next to conquer the British kingdom of Strathclyde with its capital on Dumbarton rock, and in this he failed disastrously. After his death in 761 (if not before) Dalriada recovered her independence, and the decades between then and the first attack on Iona by Vikings in 795 gave the Gaels a breathing-space of which they made effective use.

In 839 an invading Danish host inflicted a crushing defeat on the Picts, in which many of their royal house and their aristocracy were wiped out. By this time King Kenneth Mac Alpin of Dalriada was gravely menaced by Norsemen from the west and Iona lay in ruins. He therefore took advantage of Pictish weakness to move to the relative safety of the central Highlands, where relics of St Columba were

A unique hoard of Pictish silver was hidden in the Early Christian chapel on St Ninian's Isle about A.D. 800 and discovered in 1958. It probably belonged to an important and wealthy family living in Shetland who hid it from the Vikings whose raids on Northern Pictland were beginning at that time. The hoard includes twelve penannular brooches, two chapes, a spoon, a knife, a pommel, seven bowls and three curious dome-shaped objects only 40 mm high. The bases of the domes were covered then pierced with two holes suggesting they may have been buttons. Since neither Vikings nor Picts removed the treasure from its hiding place, possibly the family were victims of the raid.

brought to sanctify a new religious head-quarters at Dunkeld. From here King Kenneth set out to consolidate his power in as much of old Pictland as he could hold against the Norsemen, and thus created the kingdom of the Picts and Scots which was to survive the Viking age. In the course of these upheavals the language and institutions of the Picts gave way to those of the Gaels where they were not eliminated by the Norsemen. The Pictish symbols disappear from their stone sculpture: which lends support to the theory that these were associated in some way with ownership, and ceased to be relevant after Pictish rights in property had been lost, or when they began to be recorded in a new and alien manner.

From their islands the Norsemen assaulted the united kingdom that Kenneth Mac Alpin had founded. Evidence of the bases they established survive in such names as Ullapool on the west coast and Eriboll in the north, although there is still all too little evidence of the extent of permanent settlement as opposed to trading posts or pirates' lairs. An exceptional density of Norse names proves that the Kyle of Tongue became one of their centres, and though they did not generally penetrate far inland, this area preserves a Gaelic legend of a Norse past in Strath Uridale (now known as Strathmore) beneath Ben Hope, and at Dalrharald deep in Strath Naver. These are perhaps to be ex-plained by a Celtic resistance movement which operated from the depths of those hills and required punitive expeditions.

The relatively fertile plain of Caithness, closer to the centre of Norse power in Orkney, became the best-favoured region of mainland settlement, and here a Norse homestead has

been excavated at Freswick which reveals the same pattern of life as in the islands. But as Alan Small has pointed out, there was prob-ably one significant difference. Here, even if the natives were evicted from the most pro-ductive lands, they could at least escape from servitude into the safety of the hills. Conse-quently there is likely to have been less integration between Picts and Norsemen, either culturally or by intermarriage.

Today the county of Sutherland comprehends the whole of the northern mainland west of Caithness, but the Viking Southland was the coastal plain along the Moray Firth below the cliffs of Caithness. Here colonists who appear to have come principally from Orkney gradu-ally occupied the lands in which the superb sculptured stones of the northern Picts still stood at Golspie and Nigg and Cadboll. Between them lie the deep inlets of the Dornoch and Cromarty Firths, from where they could conveniently raid the kingdom of the Picts and Scots in the great peninsula of north-east Scotland. They established a centre that is still named Dingwall, signifying that legislative and commercial business was carried on here; yet it seems unlikely that permanent settlement in the Southland was as extensive as in the north or west.

A hoard buried at Rogart, only a few miles inland from Golspie, hints at the loot that awaited Viking raiders in this area, and the attempts made by the Picts to save their property. It includes a silver-gilt penannular brooch of Irish metalwork design with birds' heads in high relief, as though drinking out of discs at its terminals. The most spectacular buried treasure was discovered more recently 73 in the remains of a later church on St Ninian's Isle beside the Shetland mainland, placed in a wooden box beneath a stone slab inscribed with a cross. It contained three silver-gilt conical mountings intricately decorated with entwined animals, seven decorated silver bowls, and amongst other objects of superb workmanship the only silver spoon dateable to the 8th century that has ever been found in the British Isles. Since this spoon was considered to have been used for a religious purpose, it lent support to the view that this was the property of the church foundation. But experts now believe that this was secular property.

Such stray examples that have turned up in Scotland of the glittering prizes which awaited the Norse conquistadors are supplemented by those which found their way to Norway. One of the most interesting of these is an 8th century shrine that might have come from either Scotland or Ireland, and was found in north Norway in the 19th century with a Norse inscription of the 10th century carved on it: "Ranvaig owns this casket." Since it still contained its religious relics, it is possible that it was not stolen but presented to Norwegians after they had been converted. On the other hand, there are ornaments torn from reliquaries which were used to decorate horse harness, and there can be no doubt about the sacrilegious manner in which these were obtained.

The first Norse dwelling site that was found in the British Isles lies at Jarlshof near the southern tip of Shetland, and its occupation dates from the earliest period of settlement between 800 and 850. Here people had already lived for over two thousand years when the colonists erected their longhouse beside the ruins of Pictish wheel-houses. It was a rectangular dwelling 21.3 metres long by 6 metres wide, in which the ashes from the fire that burned down its centre still lay in their long trough. Its side walls curved inwards slightly at their ends; its roof had been supported by posts and rafters. Here the household cooked and ate and slept, while separate buildings, a byre, a smithy, and one that may have been the bath house stood nearby.

In this primary period of occupation the people lived by farming and animal husbandry. Although they dwelt beside a bay sheltered by surrounding headlands in which boats could be beached in safety, it was not until a later period that fishing began to play a significant part in their economy. Yet they were evidently prosperous and possessed decorated bone combs, carved pins with heads representing axes, thistles or animal heads, drew pictures of Viking longships, animals and human portraits on pieces of slate.

Before the site was discovered, A. W. Brøgger in Norway had already advanced his theory that the settlers in Orkney and Shetland were not 'bloodthirsty Viking pirates' but 'a fairly peaceful colonisation by ordinary peasants' and Jarlshof appeared at first sight to illustrate his picture. The mistake was made of supposing that these people did not possess weapons because they had not been found in middens: the only places where they are likely to have been preserved is in pagan graves, but only one of these has yet been found at Jarlshof.

F. T. Wainright was among the distinguished dark-age scholars who have tried to restore a sense of proportion (though he scotched the snake, not killed it). 'There are already one or two indications,' he wrote, 'that the men of Jarlshof had interests outside their crops and their animals. They drew pictures of boats; and they also possessed boats. And yet they were not great fishermen. Why should they want boats if not for fishing? The answer may lie in the several camp fires which were found to the north of the farmstead and which may have been lit by boat crews returning from the south, a suggestion supported by the discovery of an Irish-Scottish metal pin in the ash of one of the fires.' This is by no means the only object suggestive of a raid that the site of Jarlshof has yielded. Wainright concluded: 'it is impossible to accept Brøgger's picture of lordless, leaderless, weaponless peasants crossing the sea and setting up new homes in communities where violence and social distinctions were unknown.'

Alan Small has pointed out the variety of Viking activity, 'including individual pirate

raids, highly organised plundering, family movements for settlement, mass migration, commercial activities, and simple exploration, and it is often impossible to distinguish between them'. Small himself has excavated the farmstead of Underhoull on the island of Unst in the far north of Shetland, a much simpler unit than that of Jarlshof. But a great many more sites will have to be found and examined before the different Viking activities can be related to different parts of the Highlands and Islands in such a way as to bring that vigorous society to life once again. It is particularly necessary in the Hebrides, where only the Norse homestead at Drimore in South Uist has been investigated apart from the Udal settlement. There are strong intimations that the western isles were favoured early as a base for the assaults on Ireland which were becoming intensive from about the year 800. The wealth to be found there is well illustrated by a single hoard of ten arm-rings discovered in Ireland, which together weighed over eleven pounds of gold —the most valuable gold hoard to have come to light anywhere in Europe from the Viking Age. Yet the precise share of the Outer Hebrides in this traffic has so far proved elusive, although there are all those Norse place-names to assure us that they were galvanised into new activities during this period.

In Orkney the picture is clearer. These islands of red sandstone are exceptionally fertile and their farming potential was maintained by the new inhabitants, probably with the additional help of slave labour. Although the tides surrounding them are of such complexity, they possess safe anchorages and facilities for beaching boats, and they lay at a cross-roads of the Atlantic trade routes. By 1100 the Norwegian magnates had given up piracy in favour of legitimate trade and land development, yet the Orkney Saga states that over half a century later, Sweyn of Gairsay still divided his time systematically between agriculture and plundering. He harried as far as Ireland on his spring cruise, and embarked on a second expedition in the autumn, after the harvest had been brought in. The evidence of the sagas is not always depend-able, since they bear a resemblance to historical novels and were composed in some cases centuries after the events they relate. But the Orkney Saga was composed in about 1200, only a few decades after the career of Sweyn, and what it says on the subject may be believed. Nor can it be doubted that his pattern of life was one on which Orkney's prosperity had been based since the first settlements were made there in the years after 800.

Here, on the tidal island called the Brough of Birsay opposite the dwelling of Buckquoy, an unusual settlement grew up. Generally the pioneers of the Viking Age established themselves in quite separate farmsteads whether in Greenland, Iceland, Faroe or the Scottish isles. Each household was a self-supporting unit, although there were those such as Jarlshof which expanded with the passage of the centuries into a sizeable cluster of buildings. On the Brough of Birsay a Celtic monastery was still functioning when the 9th century opened. 'There is no suggestion', wrote Wainwright, 'that it survived the Norse immigration. The flight of the monks is perhaps best illustrated by the elaborately carved wooden box recovered from a bog in the parish of Birsay about two miles from the monastery. The designs show that it dates from the late eighth or early ninth century. It contained the tools of a woodworker, and it is not too fanciful to suggest that it was dropped by one of the community in the course of a hurried flight from the heathen marauders.'

But there were two curious developments. Although the Brough forms a rough rectangle less than half a mile in length, there was established here not merely a single longhouse of the early period, with bowed side walls as at Jarlshof, but several of them: and despite such a concentration, they were built on the slope above the remains of the religious buildings, rather than on top of them. This was the place—Birsay and its Brough—that was to become the headquarters of the Orkney earldom and the site of the first cathedral of the islands.

The date and manner of Norse conversion to Christianity in Scotland are mysteries which the recovery of Viking graves is gradually

The animal headpost from the remarkable Norwegian Oseberg ship carved by a craftsman since christened 'the Academician' because of his style. The stem post found in the island of Eigg carried no comparable decoration and of the boat in which a warrior was buried with his horse, weapons, ornaments, small balance and set of enamelled weights, beside the Bay of Kiloran, Colonsay, nothing remains but the iron rivets.

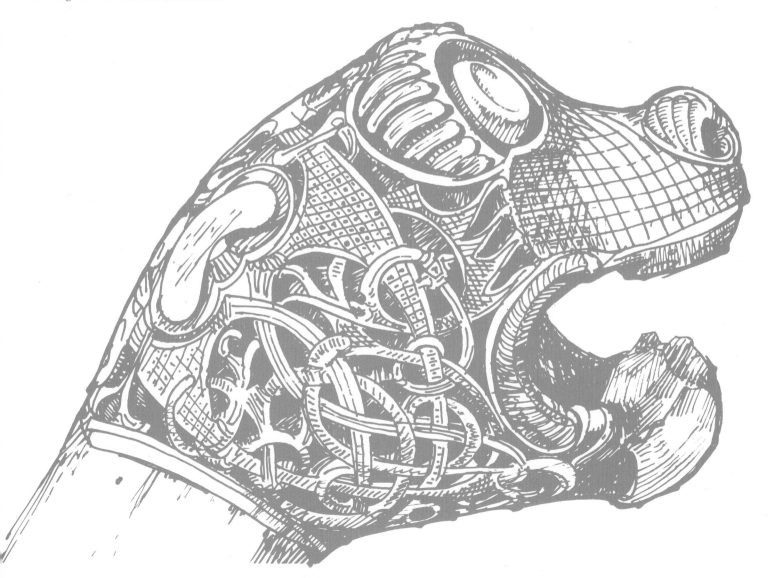

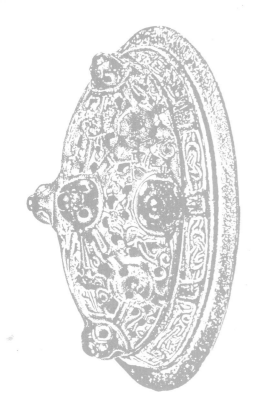

One of a pair of 9th century Norse shoulder-brooches of 'tortoise' design.

helping to solve. It is fortunate that the immigrants brought with them pagan burial practices long abandoned in Christian Pictland and Dalriada, since the grave goods belonging to these rituals reveal so much that would otherwise remain obscure. The men's graves contain the swords, spear-heads, shield-bosses and axes of people who might otherwise have been mistaken for pacific cultivators libelled by malicious clerics. The women's graves reveal how many of even the earliest immigrants brought their families with them. Characteristic accoutrements of the Norsewoman were two shoulder-brooches of a 'tortoise' design, generally in bronze, and a third brooch that could be pinned elsewhere. A beautiful example of a third brooch was found in a Viking grave at Westness in Orkney. It is circular, made of silver and gold and was fastened by means of a long pin. It is all the more interesting to us because it is of Celtic origin and must have been about a hundred years old when it was buried with its late owner. Norsewomen also wore bracelets and beads; and sometimes articles of their daily lives such as a glass linen smoother or a comb were buried with them.

These people believed in a pantheon of divinities who included Frey and his sister Freyja, god and goddess of fertility; Thor the thunder god of the sky; Odin greatest of all, god of strife and encourager of war, a fickle and terrifying figure who selected the bravest warriors to live with him in Valhall, the Hall of the Slain, where they enjoyed a life of feasting and fighting. Odin's ravens brought him information like so many carrier-pigeons, and his valkyrie maidens conducted the cream of men to Valhall at their death. Among the living Odin's initiates were the *berserkir*, which means 'bear-shirted' men who worked themselves into a frenzy in battle and howled as they entered the fray. The behaviour of these ruthless men must have contributed much to the lurid accounts of Viking barbarity. But Odin had other attributes as well. He had undergone voluntary suffering to acquire the secrets of poetry, rather as the ascetics of other religions have mortified their flesh in the quest for enlightenment, and he could bestow the gift of poetry on a human.

Besides the gods there were hosts of spirits, male and female, who remained a reality to the people of the northern isles for centuries after they had been converted to Christianity. Ernest Marwick's *The Folklore of Orkney and Shetland* shows how the supernatural folk of hill and mound and sea continued to enliven the daily round when no more than a fragmentary memory of the Norse gods remained. Only Odin, his wife Frigg and Thor have been commemorated to this day in the days of the week, since English belongs to the same Germanic family of languages as the Norse speech which it gradually displaced in the isles of the Vikings and uses the same names for Wednesday, Thursday and Friday.

Those who did not qualify for Valhall travelled after death to the underworld of the goddess Hel. In either event it was believed that they would need their personal possessions, and it looks as though some Norsemen were reluctant to deprive the dead of such comforts, even after their conversion. This is understandable. People who attribute divine power to a variety of sources find it easier to accept another, but are the harder to convince that a new god is the sole authority and means of salvation. Some Norsemen did what people have done in every age in the same predicament. Faced with the awful fact of death, they kept the options open by invoking all the supernatural aids which might prove effective.

The isle of Colonsay in the Firth of Lorne, not far across the water from Iona, had been an integral part of the kingdom of Dalriada. Its position made it an admirable base for the Viking activities of the 9th century, and here a Norse warrior received a sumptuous pagan interment in the latter half of that century, beside the bay of Kiloran. He was laid to rest in his boat with his horse, weapons and ornaments, and also a pair of bronze scales with their balance and weights. He could only have required all this gear if he hoped to be escorted to Valhall by one of the valkyries. Yet two crosses were incised on stone slabs forming part of his sepulchre, and these could only have been contributed upon the suspicion that the dead man might find himself instead before the Christian judgment seat.

Such ambivalence was not unusual. In Denmark a single soapstone mould could turn out amulets possessing both the hammer of Thor and the Christian symbol. Other Scottish evidence is only slightly less ambiguous than this. At Whiteness in Shetland a Scandinavian axe has been found in a Christian cemetery, and although it might have found its way there accidentally, it is thought more likely to have been deposited beside a Norseman at his interment, just in case he should need it after all. Ackergill in Caithness was the scene of other oddities. Here some Norse folk adopted the cist-grave rite of the Picts as well as favouring a Christian cemetery. One of their rectangular cairns contained a long cist divided by a partition in which lay a male and a female with their heads and feet facing in opposite directions. A circular cairn preserved the only relic, a bronze neck chain of Norse workmanship dating from after 900 that had been buried with a woman.

Different Norse communities seem to have adopted Christianity at different times with a varying range of conviction. Wainwright concluded that paganism did not last long in the northern isles, and that Christian influence was stronger in Orkney than in Shetland. But he had died before Anna Ritchie uncovered the pagan graves of Buckquoy in Birsay itself, one of which contained the coin of an English king who died in 956. Wainright thought it 'probable that Christianity in the Northern Isles survived the impact of the Scandinavian settlement', and decided that conversion was making headway by 850, 'and it may be that the Northern Isles were substantially Christian by 900'. Perhaps he was right, and 'these late graves', as Professor Wilson has suggested, 'indicate that the areas of Scotland settled by the Scandinavians relapsed into paganism, from which they only emerged with the conversion of Norway'. The secret lies buried in the ground, where so many Norse graves await discovery and investigation.

According to the saga evidence, the Orkney earldom officially became Christian in 995. That was the year in which Olaf Tryggvisson succeeded as King of Norway after a dramatic conversion to Christianity in the midst of his buccaneering career—possibly in the Scilly isles. Olaf encountered Sigurd, Earl of Orkney, as he was about to set out with three ships on a Viking expedition. He invited the Earl aboard his ship, and there told him bluntly: 'it is my wish that you should be baptised, and all those under you. Otherwise you will die here at once, and I shall carry fire and sword through the islands.'

Olaf used the same high-handed methods of conversion in Norway, where many of his countrymen preferred to be sent to feast with Odin in Valhall. But Sigurd accepted instant baptism, and while King Olaf does not seem to have favoured lengthy doctrinal instruction, it is doubtful whether Sigurd or his subjects stood in much need of it. In the lands of Christian Pictland which these Norsemen had been occupying by now for upwards of two hundred years, the Faith may or may not have survived without a break. Conversion of pagans may have been sporadic and subject to relapses. But by 995 Olaf Tryggvisson's ultimatum may have come as nothing more than a statement of official approval for a *fait accompli*.

As the generations succeeded one another during these two centuries other changes in society had been taking place. Traditionally the Norseman, like the Celt, had been less an individual than an integral part of a large family, whose honour, prosperity and legal obligations he shared. But the mobility of the Viking Age gradually loosened these ties, as sections of a family emigrated, and single men exchanged one loyalty for another by becoming pirates or mercenary soldiers. The bonds that united the crew of a longship might sometimes include those of family, but in many cases they would have been more comparable to those of a commercial guild.

In former times Norse family units had lived under local laws that varied from one district to another and were imposed by no distant authority. Their pagan beliefs included no concept of divine kingship such as those of the Celts, and they had developed no sense of belonging to a national entity. When the ruler of Vestfold, Harold Finehair, set out in about the year 900 to make himself sole King of 79

Norway, the farmer-fishermen and warrior chieftains expressed strong opposition, although Harold succeeded by force of arms. According to the sagas the Highlands and Islands became centres of refuge for the disaffected. 'One summer Harold Finehair sailed west to punish the Vikings, as he had grown tired of their depradations, for they harried in Norway during the summer, but spent the winter in Shetland and Orkney. He subdued Shetland and Orkney and the Hebrides, and sailed right west to the Isle of Man and laid waste the Manx homesteads.'

During this period the people here were faced by the power of two institutions of a kind that had never previously attempted to control the lives of Scandinavians, a national monarchy and an international Church. The reaction varied from one community to another, some coming to terms with these novel authorities, others resisting them. On the whole it looks as though the Norse societies of the Highlands and Islands accommodated themselves to the Church, as the better bargain of the two, but retained as much autonomy from the Norwegian kings as they could achieve. For this they required a power-centre of their own and one was provided by the Orkney earldom, which reached its zenith early in the 11th century under Thorfinn the Mighty.

During these years the Orcadians achieved a metropolitan status in the north Atlantic world such as they have never enjoyed since, though the character and attitude of the islanders is still marked by that experience. They possessed a class of 'men of property' called gæoingar, superior to the rest of the yeoman farmers either in their wealth or their kinship to the earls; and these were invested with duties of defence which included the maintenance of ships and beacons. In the early days of settlement the Norse homesteads had required nothing more than a wooden fence or a stone wall for their protection, which suggests that the average household was armed in sufficient strength to deal with a shipload of marauders. It was not until the 10th century, when the earls had a King of Norway to reckon with in addition to the Picts and Scots, that major settlements were fortified more substantially. In 995 Earl Sigurd had recently crossed to

Caithness, to fight and defeat Findlaec, ruler of Moray, when Olaf Tryggvason suddenly appeared with his menacing ultimatum.

Among the householders of average status a sense of being Orcadians, Shetlanders or Hebrideans must have grown as generation followed generation, however nostalgically some continued to remember Norway as the old homeland. The majority were odalers, the term ódal signifying a family heritage. The owner held this by inheritance, not as the representative of his kinsmen, yet he was obliged to offer them the first refusal if he wished to sell. Udal Law as it came to be called in Orkney and Shetland, survived the transfer of these islands to the Scottish crown and has helped to preserve the pattern of their societies to this day.

In the longhouses of the odalers the pagan festival feasts were probably held long after their inmates had become Christian: just as Hogmanay and Halloween are still observed throughout the Highlands, long after their ritual significance has been forgotten. The Norse observed three main feasts, at the beginning of summer, after the harvest and at midwinter. They were designed to promote safety and fertility, and auguries were sought by casting wooden chips which were then read like cards. No doubt the feasts led to much drunkenness and fighting, as dead heroes were believed to enjoy in Valhall, and as some living heroes still indulge in at Hogmanay.

Most of these people wore clothes of linen and woollen textiles, both of which became staples of the trade between Scandinavia and her far-flung settlements. Among the different techniques was one called a pile-weave, that involved tying tufts of wool round the threads to make shaggy cloaks with a texture resembling fur. Examples have been found in the Hebrides, Man and Iceland, and it was an important Icelandic export although manufactured elsewhere as well.

Over their shirts and under-pants, which might reach to their ankles, the men donned coloured tunics with a belt round the waist. Either they wore ankle-length breeches, or knee-length trousers with stockings to the knees, gartered to the leg with bands. The rich

About A.D. 700 the rather ordinary ring brooches of Scotland suddenly became highly decorative works of fine craftsmanship. The Hunterston brooch (detail, lower) marks this change. Apart from being the earliest known, it is also the most elaborate and the largest of this new jewellery, diameter 125 mm. On the back 10th–11th century runes were scratched by later owners. The Cadboll brooch from Rogart, Sutherland (above) dates from about A.D. 780. Made of silver gilt, birds' heads have been placed around the amber settings as if drinking from them.

81

displayed elaborate cuffs ornamented with embroidery or gold thread, and they also possessed cloaks with decorated borders to the hem, and trailing robes, sometimes made of silk. Poor people and slaves, by contrast, were to be seen in a blanket with a hole cut in it for the head, somewhat resembling those still worn in South America.

Women wore a chemise, sometimes pleated, beneath a long dress fastened by a belt at the waist. The sleeves of the wealthy were given a train, stiffened, or otherwise elaborated. The hair of married women was gathered up in a knot and covered by a tall head-dress, while that of maidens hung loose.

At their marriage, women undertook heavy responsibilities. Many of them were left to run isolated farms and large households for long periods while their menfolk were away, fighting or trading. The sagas tell stories about the most famous of them which help to reveal what kinds of wives were bred in the average households of that society. When Earl Sigurd was debating whether to risk crossing to the mainland, to do battle with so formidible a foe as Findlaec of Moray, his mother is said to have remarked scornfully: 'I would have reared you in my wool-basket if I had known you expected to live forever. It is fate that governs a man's life, not his own comings and goings and it is better to die with honour than live in shame.' She is typical of her kind, as they are commemorated in the sagas, despite the fact that she was the daughter of an Irish king.

According to their means they enjoyed the products both of Celtic and Norse craftsmen, weaving-tools and combs, caskets and gaming pieces. Much of the most exquisite work of the Norsemen was carved in wood. The Oseberg ship-burial in Vestfold has preserved a veritable treasure of their art from the mid-9th century—some decades before Harold Fine-hair set out from there to make himself King of Norway. The grave-goods included a cart, sledges, bed-posts and weaving implements, but the most outstanding ornaments were the stern and stem posts of the ship itself, deeply carved with interlocking animals. In Norse Scotland few of such objects have survived, and the stem post found in the island of Eigg possesses no comparable decoration. But despite the relative scarcity of wood they must have been a part of the embellishment of life here, and probably every child amused himself by carving bits of stick with his knife.

Professional tanners came into existence to meet the needs of leatherwork, as this developed into a home industry, carried out on the farm. Many utensils were made of soapstone: cooking pots and baking boards, plates and bowls, fishing weights and weaving apparatus. Since there is no soapstone in Orkney, Faroe or Iceland, this became an important export from Norway, significant for Shetland as well, where a soapstone quarry was exploited. But a side-effect of the soapstone trade was to depress the art of pottery, which had been amongst the most highly developed in the households of earlier societies.

Purchases might be paid for by such farm products as hides, woollen cloth, dried fish, butter and cheese. The small farmer could take his wares to a more substantial neighbour who traded by ship, or to a Ting if he happened to live near one. Market towns are among the most remarkable achievements of this age, but none of any significance had yet grown up in Norse Scotland. The most important commercial centre for this region was Dublin, a Norse kingdom by the time of Earl Sigurd, over which reigned Sigtrygg, son of a voluble man known as Olaf Rattle.

Purchasing power was augmented by the fruits of piracy, although a fortune could be lost by the same means that had won it in this turbulent age. The hoard of ninety silver objects found beside the bay of Skaill in Orkney is the most valuable of several that hint at the hazards of the game. Neck and arm rings, ingots, brooches and coins of English and Arabic origin had been buried in circumstances that can only be guessed before Earl Sigurd's reign began, and never been reclaimed.

Once the long, dark winter had arrived to curtail every outdoor activity, gaming boards would be set out beside the fire of the long-houses, at which men played in pairs. The beautiful chessmen of walrus ivory found in

The earliest Viking farmstead at Jarlshof was built as a two-room dwelling at the beginning of the ninth century by settlers from the Norwegian coastal districts of More-Tronde-lag; the kitchen, oven and fireplace on the left, the living room with tables, beds and a central hearth on the right. Early in the eleventh century a cattle byre with a curved entrance passage was added to the timbered east gable-end and domestic accommodation to the west. In the final phase of occupation most of this was abandoned when the west end was converted into a small two-roomed house.

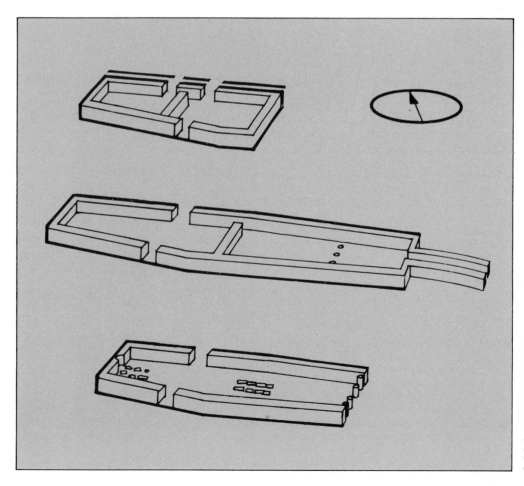

Bronze figurine from Iceland, about A.D.1000; worship of the red-bearded Thor was wide-spread. Friendlier than the mighty, fiercesome Odin, the One-eyed Frightener, Thor controlled the sun, wind and rain. Thunder was thought to be the sound of his herd of goats being driven across the sky, and lightning, the flash of his boomerang-like hammer hurled against the evil giants of the world's end.

Lewis date from a later century, but the game might have been introduced at any time after the Norse settlement began. Literacy did come late. The earliest surviving writer is Ari Thorgilsson, who composed his history a hundred years or so after Sigurd's death. Stories were told, not read, and an evening's entertainment was filled, by rich and poor alike, with recitals of poetry, the solution of riddles, exchange of scurrilous verses similar to the flyting of a later age in Gaelic and Scots.

The prince of 10th century skalds was Egil Skallagrimsson, some of whose poems were preserved by Snorri Sturluson, greatest of saga writers, over two hundred years later. It can scarcely be doubted that the poetry of Egil was heard in the hall of Sigurd, perhaps a great deal more than has survived, and the Elder Edda contains fragments of the poetry which originated in this society. The Lay of Grotti is particularly interesting. Grotti was a magic quern which could grind whatever its owner desired, and he ordered his bonds-women to turn out gold, peace and happiness. But when he would allow them no respite, they sang this lay as they ground an armed host instead. According to Snorri Sturluson, the Sea-King Mysingr then took the quern to grind salt, and when he too proved insatiable, Grotti sank his ship in the Pentland Firth and formed the whirlpool beside the isle of Stroma. This story was still remembered in South Ronaldsay in the 20th century. Another Lay, dating from the 10th century, has for its theme the unending battle in which the dead rise up each morning to fight again, and the location is the island of Hoy.

Both themes help to illuminate that age, and so does the saga story of the events leading up to the death of Earl Sigurd. At his Yule feast in 1013 Sigurd entertained King Sigtrygg of Dublin, Earl Gilli of the southern Hebrides, and several distinguished Icelanders. Among these there was Flosi, who had recently burned Njal and his family in his home, the theme of Snorri Sturluson's most famous saga. One of the Icelanders was invited to relate the grisly story for the entertainment of Sigurd's guests, and while he was doing so another who dis-agreed with his version strode to the high table and struck off his head. It was Flosi's comrade whom he had killed, yet it was Flosi who interceded for the man who had so grossly abused Sigurd's hospitality. While thralls mopped up the blood and spilt wine, Flosi explained: 'Kari has not done this without good cause. We had made no atonement with him, and what he did he had a right to do.' Kari was allowed to go free and the feast continued. Remote though these men are from the namby-pamby picture of the Viking Age, they had their own code of fair-dealing, and sometimes they honoured it.

The principal object of that gathering was to organise the enterprise of the following spring, which was nothing less than a concerted attack on Brian Boru, the High King of Ireland. One of the prizes offered to Earl Sigurd (unattractive as it appears) was the hand of Sigtrygg's mother in marriage. Her name was Kormlada, her reputation as a trouble-maker formidable: and she had once been King Brian's wife, for whom she now nursed an implacable hatred. She could scarcely have been the bait which lured Sigurd to his death in Ireland, but go he did.

The carnage of the battle of Clontarf, which was fought on Good Friday in 1014, was preceded by fearful portents. In Caithness a man called Daurrud looked through the window of a building in which he saw women working at a loom which had human heads for weights and entrails as the warp and weft. When they had completed the woof the women tore it apart and rode off with their portions, six to the south and six to the north. In Orkney a man named Hareck saw an apparition of Earl Sigurd, while elsewhere people were troubled by flocks of ravens and showers of blood. On the field Sigurd's standard-bearers were slain one after another until he seized the raven banner himself and so met his death. King Brian was killed in the hour of victory and Ireland was never again to come within sight of union under a native sovereign. But the northern earldom reached its zenith in the reign of Sigurd's son, Thorfinn the Mighty.

Earl Sigurd's mother had come from Ireland. His wife was a daughter of Malcolm II, King of what was by this time known as Alba or Scotia. So their son Thorfinn spent several formative years at the court of his grandfather King Malcolm, who lived for twenty years after Earl Sigurd had perished at Clontarf. It can hardly be doubted that he also met his uncle Findlaec, ruler of Moray, and Findlaec's son Macbeth—the cousin with whom he was to share such a long and apparently amicable association. Nor is it improbable that these contacts and intermarriages amongst the top people illustrate a process of fusion that was far advanced throughout the Highlands and Islands by the 11th century.

Moray was what remained of the old northern Pictish kingdom. When Columba had visited King Brudei in the 6th century, its control extended as far as the northern isles and the outer Hebrides. Findlaec's realm was smaller, but it still reached from Drumochter in the south to the Dornoch Firth, where it faced the Norse Sutherland. The Irish annals continued to define the ruler of Moray as a King; but in the year 918 the earliest surviving reference occurs to the title Mormaer. Its meaning is not beyond dispute, but it is thought to define the office of a Sea Steward and the territory of Morven in the west may mean Mormaer's land. Suffice to say, this was another territory like Moray in which the ruler's heaviest responsibility was to guard the coasts from Norse attack. From 918 onwards the rulers of Moray were called Mormaers as well as kings. Inland, the kingdom of Moray ended at the river Oykell. Since the Norsemen seem to have maintained no more than isolated settlements along the mainland coast to the west, such as Tongue and Eriboll, there were large hinterlands of the northern Highlands which were probably populous with the descendants of Pictish refugees of the Viking Age, and perhaps of Kenneth Mac Alpin's conquests also. Close to the stones of Dalharald by the Naver river lies the deserted township of Rossal, with its earth-house of pre-Norse times and its relics of mediaeval occupation. Had it been abandoned in the interval as a place too vulnerable to attack from Naver-mouth, where boats could so conveniently be beached? At any rate,

there were plenty of inaccessible glens in that neighbourhood where a sizeable population could live sumptuously on fish and game, besides raising a few crops, and raiding Norse farmsteads when the men were away at sea.

One of the reasons why so little is known about the original inhabitants during this period is that their principal language disappeared in the course of it, without a single complete sentence surviving: and oral tradition depends entirely on the survival of the language in which it is transmitted unless it has been committed to writing. The Gaels did this, preserving traditions that reached back to pre-Christian times as well as keeping contemporary records. The Norse did the same later, enshrining their traditions in an immense saga literature. But if any Pict attempted it, his labours have been lost.

After people have lost their traditions with their language, they are apt to adopt the legends of the speech which replaces it. The Gunn clan, for instance, has been credited with descent from a man of the Norse sagas named Gunni, and also with the supposition that its name derives from the Norse word for war, Gunnr. These theories are mutually exclusive, but they share an assumption that the Gunns, found in historical times in the area north of the Helmsdale river, were of Norse origin.

This territory does fall within the Norse earldom of Caithness, but it contains the massif of Morven and the Scarabens, a barrier behind which the natives of northern Pictland would have done well to retire when Viking raiders and settlers moved into their relatively fertile coastlands. It is at least as plausible to assume that the Gunns are of Pictish origin, although the disadvantage follows that there are no Pictish sagas or language in which to delve in search of a derivation for the name. Neil Gunn, the most significant writer in the history of the Highlands, had an instinctive belief that this was so, and it exercised a profound influence on his compositions.
Pre-Pictish peoples and cultures must not be forgotten either, for their threads are woven into the region's tapestry, however obscurely. The name of the Naver river has been given

both a Gaelic and a Norse original, more mutually exclusive than Gunni and Gunnr, and less likely than either. The alternative assumption, that it survives from some lost aboriginal language, as river names are especially likely to do, is once again unattractive, since it provides no identifiable embroidery.

Along the western seaboard, the three hundred mile chain of islands that stretch from the Calf of Man to the Butt of Lewis, there lived the mixed race of people who became known as Gall Ghaidheil, meaning Foreigner-Gaels. Obviously their composition varied from one island to another, while it appears that the mainland Gaels retained much of their integrity as far north as Ardnamurchan throughout the age of amalgamation and transition. It was from this heartland that the Gaelic language eventually flowed back, as Norse influence waned, even to the long island of the Outer Hebrides where it had never previously taken deep root.

There was a two-way process of enrichment. Double-walled black houses were built for centuries after the Viking age to Norse design, and as late as the 18th century the rectangular long-houses of tacksmen and ministers in the Highlands resembled those in which Norsemen had lived at the upper end, while the other was used as a byre for the cattle. Everywhere the evidence suggests that Norsemen continued the agricultural practices that they found wherever they settled with little alteration; but they must have revolutionised the local skills in seamanship. The Hebrides belonged to a kingdom of the Sudreys or Southern Isles which included Man, and we know that Man was required to supply crews for about sixteen ships of 40 oars or twenty-four ships of 26 oars, as their contribution to naval defence. Whatever the Hebridean quota may have been, it was the founding of a tradition that flowered in the achievements of the birlinn or war galley of a later age, such as the Gaelic poem of about 1310 celebrated:

Tryst of a fleet against Castle Sween:
Welcome is the adventure in Ireland;
Norsemen travelling the billows;
Brown barks are being cleansed for them.
Tall men are arraying the fleet

Which swiftly holds its course on the sea's bare surface.
No hand lacks a trim warspear
In battle of targes, polished and comely.
Of quilted hauberks is arrayed
The bark's forefront in form of jewels,
Of warriors with brown-faced girdles.
They are Norsemen and nobles.

In the realm of the Gall Ghaidheil the war galley was commemorated in stone sculpture and in heraldry, and in poetry as late as that of Alasdair Mac Mhaigstir Alasdair and Rob Donn in the 18th century.

Of the arts which mingled in the melting-pot, one that had been outstanding became lost. By 1000 those masters of stone sculpture, the Picts, had 'lost all trace of their individuality', as the expert on their work, Robert Stevenson, has written. The marvellous woodwork of the Norwegians has not survived in the Scottish climate and soil, if it was executed or imported here, while their conversion to Christianity does not seem to have inspired many stone monuments of Scandinavian design, although there are a few tell-tale carvings. One found at Kibar on the isle of Barra is drawn from a Manx model—not very skilfully. Another from Islay, now in Edinburgh possesses scroll-work resembling that of Ringerike, a Norse style that was brought to its highest excellence by Irish craftsmen. Perhaps other finds will be made to tell us more about the part which Hebrideans played in the exchange of ideas between Norway and the kingdom of Dublin.

The earliest Norse writings in Scotland take the form of runic inscriptions, and the first in date to have been discovered is inscribed on the early 8th-century brooch found at Hunterston on the coast of Ayrshire. The writing has been dated to the 10th century, but the man it commemorates has the Celtic name Melbride and the jewel is Celtic also. For the rest, the runic inscriptions are later. A particularly interesting one was carved on a funeral slab on Iona, with an interlaced cross. It reads: 'Kali Auiusson laid this stone over Fugl his brother.' This belongs either to the 11th or to the 12th century. The largest single collection of runic inscriptions found anywhere in Europe can be dated to the middle of the 12th, and was incised on the chamber-walls of Maes Howe in Orkney after Vikings had broken into the tomb.

But interesting though these mementoes are, they are not comparable to the surviving writings of the Gaels in the same period. These are preserved in the Book of Deer, a volume of gospel passages in Latin ornamented with full-page pictures of the apostles, and designs like those of the greater masterpieces of the Celtic church. But around the year 1100, Gaelic entries were added, the first of which tells the legendary story of the founding of the monastery of Deer some five hundred years earlier. Columba, it relates, came from Iona with his disciple Drostan to a place that "was pleasing to Columcille because it was full of God's grace". After he had cured a sick son of the local ruler by his prayers, this man donated the property for a monastery, in which Columba left Drostan as abbot. When Drostan shed tears at Columba's departure, the saint said: 'Let Deer be its name hence-forth'—Deur being the Gaelic for a tear.

Subsequent entries describe a society that was by now wholly Gaelic, although it lay in Buchan in the extreme north-east of former Pictland, a far cry from Irish Dalriada. So they can be taken as describing the way of life throughout the lands between, as it had evolved centuries before. Apart from a few biblical names such as Andrew and Samson and David, all are Gaelic, and the relation of the rulers to the governed is defined in unique detail. There was the High King, the Mormaers next in rank, and beneath these the Toisich or district chiefs. The office of Toiseach was to survive in the clan name Mackintosh, and in the Book of Deer we learn of one Toiseach of the kindred of Cano, another of the kindred of Morgann.

The freemen were organised in units of households and townships upon which taxes were levied collectively. These were paid in kind, since there was as yet no Scottish coinage, to the King, Mormaer and Toiseach, as well as to the church. They were based on the Davach, a fiscal unit reckoned by the number of cattle that a piece of ground was able to support, together with its arable yield.

The davach was to retain its place in the Highland economy for centuries to come. Duties of service and supply were also exacted by rulers and churchmen as they travelled about the land, and there were fixed obligations of military service.

The Book of Deer preserved such details inasmuch as they related to a particular monastic property. In these days before the introduction of parishes, the monasteries had become an integral part of the patriarchal structure. Every tribe had its monastery and its abbot was a member of the ruling family. Since there was no law of celibacy for men in holy orders, the office had naturally become hereditary. Some abbots remained laymen, though they might still administer large properties; and in relatively barren regions these might possess an enormous acreage, such as was necessary to support a religious community.

That of St Maelrubha at Applecross stretched from Loch Duich to Loch Broom, and was administered by a family who became known as MacTaggarts, Sons of the Priest, one of whom was eventually invested as Earl of Ross. The monastery of St Fillan owned Glen-dochart and Glenfalloch, and it is thought that the MacNabs, Sons of the Abbot, originated here. The Mackinnons derive their name from Fingon of the royal house, and descend from the founder's kin of Iona. In fact the last abbot of Iona, who died in 1500 and whose effigy may still be seen there, was Iain Mackinnon.

For information about how Gaelic people dressed in this age we look to Ireland. Clothing is described amply in contemporary Irish literature, and beautifully illustrated in Irish art. Its most extraordinary feature, already alluded to, is that it did not follow the fashion of other northern Europeans, but continued that of the Greeks and Romans in the Mediterranean world. Reference has been made in an earlier chapter to the léine, the garment usually described in English as a shirt; which men wore either to the knee, to the calf, or to the ankle. Women always wore it full-length. When Gaels referred to the léine in Latin, they used the word tunica, which defined the similar garment worn by the Romans, so if the English word tunic is understood in this sense, it serves better than the word shirt. When the tunic was worn short by a man, his legs were generally left bare between the knees and the shoes, as by the Romans.

Over the tunic was worn a Brat, a term that the Gaels did not trouble to define as a curious stranger might have done, though their references do disclose that it was four-cornered, whether or not it was square in shape. As to its size, there is mention of a woman riding in a chariot whose brat trailed on the ground behind her, but presumably they were not all as capacious as this. The garment has been called a mantle in English, and to some extent it corresponded with the Roman toga. It was fixed by a pin at the shoulder or chest, and possessed neither sleeves nor hood. The only addition to these two garments, which formed the dress of men and women alike, was the Criss, which means a belt or girdle. It encircled the tunic and was used to carry weapons, books, purse, even the little harp known as a clarsach.

The tunic was rarely fashioned of undyed silk; more often of bleached linen, often described as 'bright'. The mantle was almost always described as having some definite colour, and possessed decorated borders and corners, which probably represented the status of different professions. White distinguished the cleric and the monk. The figures in the Book of Kells reveal how colourful the costume must have appeared, while the shrine of St Moedoc in Ireland reveals in skilful detail how the draperies were arranged both by men and by women.

This was the costume of the aristocracy, and it served to distinguish them from the Norsemen as unmistakably as the differences between the Celtic and Norse languages. Indeed, when a Norwegian King adopted it, his eccentricity served to invest him with the nickname by which he was remembered, and which a saga later explained as follows. 'It is said that when King Magnus returned from this expedition to the west, he adopted the costume in use in the western islands, and likewise many of his followers; that they went barelegged, having short tunics and also upper garments. And so many people called him Barelegged or Barefoot.' The date of this expedition by Magnus Barelegs was 1093.

The lesser folk of Gaeldom wore clothing like that of the Norsemen, the costume that the Romans had described as almost universal among the barbarians of northern Europe. It consisted of jacket and breeches or trews, which might either be tight-fitting or baggy like trousers, and either long or short. It descended, in fact, from the dress of Celtic Europe in an earlier age. Sometimes a small kind of brat or mantle was added. Curiously, it was the trews worn by the lower orders during this period that had come into favour amongst the Highland aristocracy by the 18th century; while a skirt reaching to the knee (if not even shorter) had become the universal costume of their clansmen, in the form of the belted plaid.

The society of Norseman and Gael, the mixed stock known as the Gall Ghaidheil, and that of the submerged Picts, was moving by the 11th century into a state of equilibrium. Both Norse and Gaelic institutions were developing autonomously within the region, their cultures fertilised and underpinned by those of Ireland on the one hand and of Norway on the other. But during this century a series of events occurred that were to set the people of the Highlands and Islands on a different course, one that even the most far-sighted would have found it hard to predict.

The first of these was the battle of Clontarf in 1014 in which King Brian of Ireland was killed, leaving no effective leader to succeed him. The cradle of Scottish civilisation, to which the Norsemen had contributed such a remarkable commercial centre at Dublin, would be the first of the two flanking bastions to fall.

A second set of circumstances brought the danger much nearer home. Earl Thorfinn's grandfather Malcolm II, King of Scotia, took some extremely brutal steps to alter the succession to his crown. Ever since the reign of Kenneth Mac Alpin it had passed by the law of tanistry, which was designed to ensure 89

Runic inscriptions on the chamber walls of Maes Howe date from the middle of the twelfth century A.D. when Vikings broke into the neolithic tomb in search of treasure.

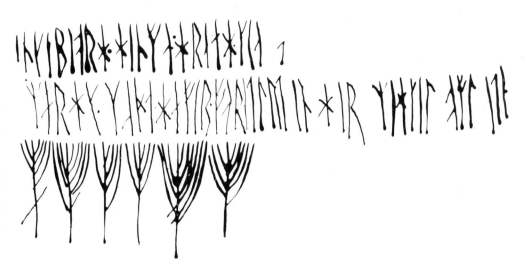

'Ingibjorg hin fahra aehkia a morhg kona, haefir farit lut in hir mikil oflati'
'Ingibjorg, the fair widow. Many a haughty woman has stooped to walk in here.'

Ingibjorg was quite a common name. Perhaps the writer, slighted or ignored by the beautiful widow, was thinking of the way she would have to stoop or unbend in the chambers and passage of the tomb, or possibly, how the grave more generally speaking is a great leveller.

'That man sat ir ekiae he at feuar abrot, thrim notom uarfi brot fort haeltr Ænthaeir'

'The man who sat here in sorrow. He broke forth from the treasure guard; with three comrades from the stronghold broke forth the hero Ænthaeir'

This inscription appears on a single, relatively narrow, corner buttress stone and is here read from right to left; the first character on the right is meaningless and is probably the result of the writer 'trying his hand'. He was most probably British rather than Norse to judge by his use of words.

Above

'Sia houghr uar fyrlathin haeltr, Thaeir uoro huater slithu oro, Ut northr er olghit mikit that uar'

'This howe was quite abandoned. Away to the north much treasure is buried. That was in Ronaldsay'

Above right

'Lothbroka synar ghaenar, Maen saem thaeir uoro fyri sir, Iorsalafarar brutu Orkough—Lifmut sa li ai aris loftir—Hir uar fi folghit mikit (raeist) sael er sa er fina, Ma than outh hin mikla, Oko Naekn bar firr oughi thisum'

'Lothbrok's sons, what doughty men they were. Crusaders broke open Ork-howe—shelter mount; but this foreboding retreat still stands. Here much treasure was buried. Happy is he who may find that great wealth. Otho was carried past this howe in the ship Naern.'

'Vemund raest'
'Vemund carved (these runes)'

91

that the heir was a senior member of the royal house, and never a minor. Anyone was eligible whose father, grandfather or great-grandfather had been a king, and not once had the immediate descendant of a king succeeded directly at his father's death. The crown had passed invariably among the collatoral branches, and it was this very practice that had enabled Malcolm II to succeed in 1005 as the representative of a junior branch, following a king of the senior line (whom he had murdered).

King Malcolm determined that in future the succession should pass exclusively through his own descendants, and he set out to ensure this by killing all the senior heirs, so effectively that when he died in 1034 there were none left, except by descent through a woman. On the other hand Malcolm himself left only daughters, so that his grandsons based their claim on female descent also.

The tanist of the senior line was Lulach, son of Princess Gruoch, granddaughter of a king and sole survivor of Malcolm's purge. But Lulach was still a child, so that his claim would have to wait in favour of that of the senior adult tanist who was Macbeth, son of Findlaec of Moray and nephew of Malcolm II. What made his claim all the stronger was that he had married Gruoch after she was widowed: her first husband was probably one of King Malcolm's victims. If the new law of succession was preferred, then the senior heir was Malcolm's grandson Earl Thorfinn of Orkney. Why Macbeth and Thorfinn did not intervene to secure the crown for one or the other of them remains a mystery. Apparently without opposition from either it passed instead to Duncan, evidently a favourite, for whom his grandfather Malcolm had already secured the crown of Strathclyde, the old British kingdom which had been assaulted in vain in the past. The succession of Duncan was to prove one of the most fateful events in the history of the Highlands.

Duncan was the son of Malcolm's daughter Bethoc and her husband Crinan, hereditary abbot of Dunkeld. Once the Fortress of the Caledonians as its name implied, subsequently the headquarters of the Columban church, Dunkeld's monastery had grown rich in territorial possessions, its abbot an eligible husband for the king's daughter. To the south lay Strathclyde, and King Duncan tried by force to extend his kingdom even further south. Initially he does not seem to have interfered with his cousins of Moray or Orkney beyond the barrier of the Mounth, nor they with him. But after Duncan had been defeated in his aggressions against his southern neighbours, he involved himself in a quarrel with Thorfinn the Mighty.

The Orkney earldom belonged to the sovereignty of Norway: that of Caithness with its Sutherland to the Scottish crown. Duncan demanded tribute for the Caithness earldom and when Thorfinn refused it, he brought an army north to fight his cousin. It remains open to question whether the Orkney saga, composed in Iceland about a hundred and fifty years later, gives an accurate account of what followed despite the fact that it called King Duncan 'Karl'. It says that 'he raised the army from the whole of the south of Scotland, both from the east and from the west, and south as far as Kintyre. The whole army he summoned against Earl Thorfinn, and they met at Tarbetness in the south of the Moray Firth. There was a great battle, and the Scots had by far the larger army. Karl had his standard borne against Thorfinn. There was then a great struggle; and the upshot was that Karl took to flight; but some men say that he was killed.'

Duncan was certainly killed, after a reign of six years, in 1040. A contemporary Irish annalist confirms what one might assume, that he was still a very young man: 'Duncan, Crinan's son, sovereign of Scotland, was slain by his subjects at an immature age.' Another Irish scholar suggested that it was not Thorfinn who killed Duncan. His name was Marianus Scotus, and he became a monk in Cologne a year before Macbeth's death, so that the record of events that survives in his own hand carries weight as hearsay. 'Duncan the King of Scotland,' Marianus believed, 'was killed by his Mormaer Macbeth, Findlaec's son, who succeeded to the kingdom and reigned for seventeen years.'

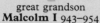

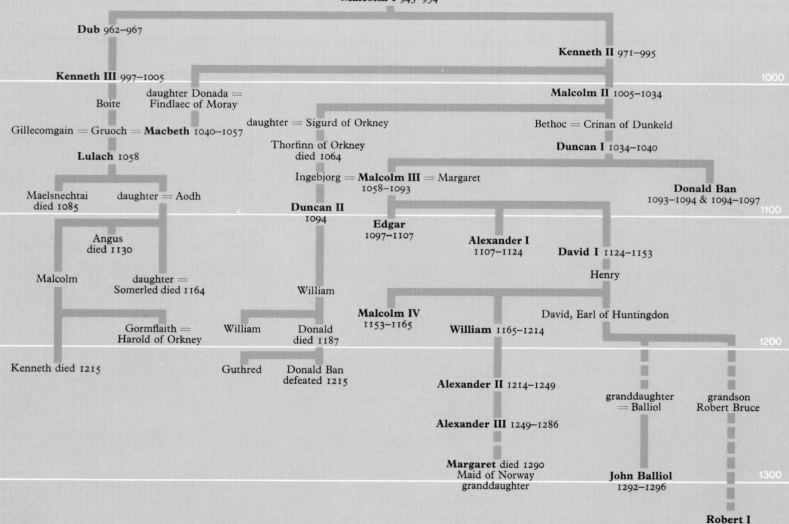

If the battle was fought at Tarbetness in Easter Ross (and this would appear to be in the south to someone writing in the north), then Duncan never penetrated into Thorfinn's earldom at all, but perished in Moray. The Chronicle of Melrose, which is even later than the Orkney Saga, names the very spot as a smith's bothy—Both na Gowan. Between these scraps of evidence and the fabrications adopted (not invented) by Shakespeare, there lies an ocean of conjecture. But the real significance of Duncan's futile venture was that it set a pattern for the centuries ahead, in which Kings of Scots mobilised forces from outside the Highlands and Islands to destroy their autonomy.

Now Lulach the senior heir was still only eight years old. Duncan had left two sons who must have been even younger. The succession lay exactly where it had done at Malcolm II's death, between Thorfinn as descendant and Macbeth as tanist. The old law prevailed when Macbeth succeeded as High King of Scots, presumably by agreement with Thorfinn, and if the Melrose Chronicle is to be believed, 'in his reign there were productive seasons.' During this period Earl Thorfinn made a pilgrimage to Rome, and Marianus Scotus noted that his cousin did the same. 'The King of Scotland, Macbeth, scattered money like seed to the poor of Rome.' He also made religious endowments within his kingdom, of which the record of one survives. 'For prayers and intercessions, Macbeth son of Findlaec and Gruoch daughter of Boite, High King and Queen of Scots, granted to Almighty God and to the Culdees of the island of Loch Leven, Kyrkness with its boundaries.' This is the earliest recorded act of a Queen Regnant in Scottish history.

The benefactions of Thorfinn were recalled in the statement that 'he sat almost always in the district of Birsay (*i byrgisheraoi*), and let them build there Christchurch, a splendid minster.' This church was erected into a cathedral during the following century, with Bishop William as its first prelate, and from the year 1154 it belonged to the archbishopric of Trondheim in Norway. It has now been accepted for several decades that excavations on the Brough of Birsay have uncovered the remains of the cathedral of Christchurch, standing on the site of the older Celtic monastery below the slope occupied by Norse longhouses. A complex of low walls beyond have been identified as the episcopal palace of Bishop William and the earlier hall of Earl Thorfinn. The hall was built so near the cliff-edge that much of its structure has been carried away by erosion.

These interpretations rest on the high authority of Stewart Cruden and C. A. R. Radford, while the Orcadians have preserved traditions so ancient and persistent that they must also be considered. These place both Christchurch and the palaces on the mainland, on a site not yet excavated, although stones containing fluted window-facings and at least one episcopal memorial have come to light there over the years. It lies beside a burn-mouth accessible to boats, whereas the Brough opposite is a rock-girt tidal island possessing no such amenity. This might be all very well for the farming peasantry of the Brough's longhouses, but it was not the kind of site generally favoured by the warrior aristocracy of that society. Neither do the saga references mention the Brough, although these generally show a detailed knowledge of the topography of Orkney. One would expect this knowledge to be most exact when it concerned the seat of the earl and the bishop, and indeed the term 'district of Birsay' is used invariably.

R. G. Lamb has suggested recently that in any case the remains on the Brough do not correspond to the 'splendid minster' of the saga. The nave of the church is only twenty-nine feet long by sixteen in width: it possesses a choir less than eleven feet square with a little apse behind, and although its layout and size are comparable to those of the episcopal seat at Gardar in Greenland, it is odd that islands with an architectural tradition unique in Europe, and now at the height of their prosperity, should have produced nothing more impressive than the settlers did in remote and inhospitable Greenland. Lamb concludes that the Brough's ruins are the chapel and other premises of a Norse monastery, and that Christchurch and the palaces lie unexplored where local tradition has placed them. Of

The coronation of Macbeth

Hardly the tyrant of 'detestable cruelties' recorded by Raphael Holingshed in his Chronicles of the late sixteenth century nor the villain of Shakespeare's essentially Jacobean play, Macbeth ruled for seventeen years 'liberal, secure and a great benefactor of the Celtic Church. Born in 1005, his claim to the throne under the rule of tanistry was as good as that of his slightly older cousin Duncan who succeeded in 1034. Six years later Macbeth asserted his claim by force of arms and Duncan was killed in battle.'

course when the site is excavated, it may simply vindicate the case for the Brough.

Had the government of the Highlands and Islands remained locally based, in the hands of Thorfinn's and Lulach's descendants, their subsequent history might have been very different. But the late King Duncan had left two baby sons, at least one of whom was carried to England where he was reared in a foreign environment as a useful pawn. He was known as Malcolm Ceann Mór or Canmore (meaning Big Head but probably better translated as Great Headman or Great Chief), and as soon as he was old enough, Edward of England and Siward of Northumbria invaded Scotland in his name. From 1054 King Macbeth met their aggressions with varying success, until in 1057 he was killed near Lumphanan in Mar. Lulach was now twenty-six years old and was accordingly invested as High King of Scots, but as Marianus noted in Cologne: 'Findlaec's son was killed in August. Lulach succeeded him and was killed in March, and Malcolm succeeded him.' The Irish annalist stated that Malcolm slew him 'by treachery', while the Chronicle of the Scottish Kings adds the detail that 'he was killed in Essie in Strathbogie and was buried in the island of Iona.' Thus, just over two centuries since Kenneth Mac Alpin had extended the rule of a resident Gaelic monarchy throughout the Highlands, it was replaced by one whose centre and source of power lay outside them to the south. This dynasty likewise endured for two hundred years, during which it succeeded step by step in undermining the native Norse and Gaelic authorities throughout the north, and substituting its own.

After the fall of Lulach, it looks as though Malcolm III did his best to placate such a powerful rival to his throne as Thorfinn of Orkney. He married the earl's daughter Ingebjorg, who was his second cousin, and begot a son named Duncan as his heir before his queen died. Thorfinn lived until 1065, when he was said by the saga to have held nine earldoms, all the Hebrides and a slice of Ireland. Even if this was an exaggeration, he does appear to have received a golden handshake.

In the year after his death there occurred a distant event that was to have profound consequences in the north. William of Normandy invaded and conquered England in 1066. He belonged to the mixed race of Franks and Norsemen who had established a province of the Northmen or Normans in France, and he brought in his wake men whose names survive to this day throughout the region; Sinclair, Bruce and Comyn, Stewart, Fraser and Menzies. The immediate effect of King William's take-over was to send the victims of his conquest scurrying for asylum to Scotland, and among them was Edgar the Atheling or claimant to the English throne, and his sister Margaret. Sometime between 1068 and 1070 the widowed King Malcolm married Margaret, with consequences that were to be equally far-reaching for the Highlands.

For Margaret was an exceedingly masterful woman, and one of her most conspicuous achievements was to undermine the authority of the native Celtic church whose roots lay in Gaeldom, and substitute that of York and Canterbury. Her success earned her this tribute from the Anglo-Saxon Chronicle. 'The prescient Creator knew beforehand what he would have done by her. For she was to increase the praise of God in the land, and direct the King from his erroneous path and incline him, together with his people, to a better way, and suppress the evil habits which the nation had previously cultivated.' One of the prospects of this better way was the claim of the See of York that the whole of Scotland lay within its diocese.

During the long reign of Malcolm III and Queen Margaret the descendants of Thorfinn in Orkney and of Lulach in Moray appear to have been left undisturbed while the King engaged in successive campaigns against William of England, the enemy of his wife's house. This caused a crisis in 1072 when William invaded Scotland and penetrated as far as Abernethy, where he not only compelled Malcolm to accept him as his feudal overlord, but took away Duncan his heir as a hostage. Perhaps this did not distress Queen Margaret, who had borne a son named after her brother the Atheling—an auspicious alternative to Ingebjorg's son.

In the seventeenth and eighteenth centuries a number of apocryphal portraits of the early Scottish kings were painted and engraved including one of Malcolm III, Canmore or Ceann Mor, 1058–1093, that fierce unlettered warrior. His second wife, Margaret, a devout, cultivated if strong-minded woman influenced a policy which was Anglo-Norman and anti-Celtic. She was canonised in 1251 a hundred and fifty years after her death.

But when Malcolm III was killed near Alnwick in 1093 during an invasion of England, neither of them at first succeeded to his crown. Margaret died soon after learning her husband's fate, and then there was a strong revulsion against the English influence at court which had found such a powerful supporter in her. Malcolm's younger brother Donald Bàn was invested as king by the law of tanistry in what amounted to a Celtic revival, as the Anglo-Saxon Chronicle noted. 'The Scots chose as King Donald, Malcolm's brother, and drove out all the English who were with King Malcolm before.' But the Norman regime in England had not made a feudal vassal of King Malcolm and taken possession of his heir for nothing. They brought him to Scotland with an Anglo-Norman army, where he was accepted 'on the condition that he should never again introduce English or French into the land.'

The terms proved impossible to fulfil: there was another Celtic reaction in a matter of months, when Duncan II was deposed and killed, and Donald Bàn restored to the throne. But Duncan's death was all that his step-brother Edgar required to stake his own claim to the throne. In 1097, once again by means of Anglo-Norman arms, Edgar deposed Donald Bàn, whom he blinded, and so established the Margaretson dynasty on the Scottish throne. This name has been bestowed on it by Professor Gordon Donaldson, and it is an exact one since the true line of Malcolm Canmore descended from his eldest son Duncan II.

So far as the people of the Highlands and Islands were concerned, the Margaretsons did not possess the shadow of a legitimate claim, besides being essentially foreign, and dependent on foreign arms. The senior representative of the royal house until his death in 1085 was their resident king, Lulach's son, who appears to have fared better than some of his relatives according to the Annals of Ulster: 'Maelsnechtai, Lulach's son, the King of Moray, happily ended his life.' Since he left no children his heir was his sister, whose husband Aodh ruled *jure uxoris* over Moray as the first to be invested with the title of Earl. Since he witnessed the charters of a King of Scots, it

can be presumed that his position was regarded at court with some deference.

The Gaelic for the Sons of Aodh, Mhic Aoidh, has been anglicised to Mackay or MacHeth, although the Irish form Magee represents the sound better in English phonetics. Aodh's sons and grandsons were the last eligible, as grandsons and great-grandsons of King Lulach, to succeed as representative of the senior line of the royal house, and they were supported by the people of Galloway and Argyll, as well as those of Moray, in the Highland resistence movement to the usurping dynasty. After they had failed, their descendants continued the struggle in the name of the alternative line of Duncan II. It was not until 1230 that the last legitimate heir was murdered by the Margaretsons.

Queen Margaret was canonised in 1251. Her contemporary Queen Gruoch, from whom the true line descended, was consigned to oblivion from which an imaginative historian of Aberdeen rescued her in the 16th century, giving her the credit for Macbeth's seizure of the crown. 'His wife lay sore upon him to attempt the thing, as she that was very ambitious, burning in unquenchable desire to bear the name of a queen.' Such are the rewards of success and failure.

Throughout the 12th century the native rulers in the Norse territories maintained their rule with occasional interference by kings of Norway and only the slightest contacts with kings of Scots. This was the long golden summer which the people of Orkney and Shetland still recall with pride, commemorated by some of the finest architecture in the islands and made vivid in saga story.

One of the most tremendous incidents in it, deeply moving the hearts of ordinary people, was a murder that took place on the 16th April 1117 in the little isle of Egilsay. The victim was Earl Magnus, one of Thorfinn's grandsons, treacherously done to death there by a rival cousin. When Magnus found himself cornered, and the man who was ordered to kill him shed tears at the horror of his task, Magnus comforted him, saying: 'Stand before me and hew a great wound in my head, for it is not right to put me to death like a thief. 97

Be of good heart, poor man, for I have prayed to God that he be merciful to you.' After his death, the corpse of Magnus was taken to Christchurch, where many others came to beg for his intercession, with such results that he was canonised. The place that St Magnus came to occupy in the hearts and lives of the islanders has been expressed by George Mackay Brown like this.

"What did they bring to the saint?
The shepherds a fleece.
That winter many lambs were born in the
    snow.
What did the dark ones bring?
To Magnus the tinkers have brought
A new bright can. Their hammers beat all
    night.
What have they brought to the saint?
A fishless fisherman
Spread his torn net at the door of the church
And the farm boys offered
A sweetness, gaiety, chastity
Of hymning mouths.
The women came to the martyr
With woven things
And salt butter for the poor of the island.
And the poor of the island
Came with their hungers,
Then went hovelwards with crossed hands
    over the hill."

These words remind us of what is missing from the saga story, what is generally so hard to find in historical records, the feelings and experience of ordinary people. A rare glimpse of a fishless fisherman is given in the Orkney Saga, but only because an earl crossed his path. This was Rognvald, the nephew of St Magnus, who had been wrecked on the coast of Shetland on his way back from Norway. Near Sumburgh, where the inhabitants of that prosperous farmstead at Jarlshof were turning with increasing enthusiasm to the fisheries, Earl Rognvald encountered an old man who sat anxiously beside his boat, unable to put to sea because his companion had not turned up to assist him. Rognvald (who had dressed in commoner's clothes since his accident) offered to accompany him instead, and terrified the old man by rowing straight into the dangerous waters of the roost. But

they returned safely with an excellent catch, and then Rognvald extemporised some verses which gave away his identity.

The incident is a reminder of the amenities of local rule. However unworthy some bosses might be, they were closely integrated with their subjects, shared their culture and could understand their needs. A distant administration, as the Highlands and Islands were to discover to their irreparable loss, generally did neither. Rognvald could joke in verse with poor fisherfolk, and could row their boats at least as well as they could. He linked their environment with Norway and with Byzantium. He gave the islanders no less a monument than the cathedral of St Magnus at Kirkwall. They believed in him to the extent that he too was canonised before the century was out. This was the asset that the Norse inhabitants of the region still possessed, while the Gaels fought their losing battle to recover it.

Work began on the new cathedral in 1137, at a time when the whole of Scotland contained only two other buildings of comparable magnificence—at Dunfermline and Kelso—and these too were under construction. The King responsible was Margaret's youngest and ablest son David I, who enjoyed the advantage that he had been the premier baron of England until he inherited the Scottish crown, and was able to bring north with him a galaxy of talented Anglo-Normans to run the institutions of church and state. With his more limited resources, Earl Rognvald helped to finance his undertaking by allowing the odalers to buy the titles to their lands outright. He also took a share of the loot brought home by that latter-day Viking pirate, Sweyn of Gairsay.

Rognvald himself went on the most colourful expedition of all. It was described as a crusade, and even if it was no more of a piratical raid than most of the others were, it was certainly no less. They won the jack-pot too, a prince's treasure in a captured vessel. But they looted the ship and then set her on fire without having found it, and only discovered their loss when a stream of precious molten metal flowed, hissing, into the sea.

Rognvald was canonised in 1192 when Bjarni of Wyre was bishop, a poet whose Lay of the Jomsvikings has survived. Rognvald was followed by Harold Maddadson, who married Gormflaith, granddaughter of Aodh and King Lulach's daughter. For her, Earl Harold espoused the legitimist cause of the Gaels, and as a punishment the King of Scots took Sutherland from his earldom of Caithness, and placed one of his own henchmen in this northern outpost of royal authority. The line of the Norse earls of Orkney ended in 1231 with the death of Earl Harold's son John, and that was the year after the cause of Duncan II's descendants was wiped out in a final rising. The feudal order crept north from Sutherland to Caithness and the islands beyond.

In the time of Earl Rognvald the Gall Ghaidheil of the west found a formidable leader. His name was Somerled, derived from the Norse for Summersailor, while both his father and his grandfather possessed Gaelic names. At first he recognised the overlordship of David I, King of Scots, as he gradually cemented his position in Argyll, then extended his control northwards until it reached the ancient boundary of the Ardnamurchan peninsula. In 1156 he established his supremacy in the island world as well by defeating the Norse king of the western isles and Man in a hard-fought sea-battle. He married a granddaughter of King Lulach, and so joined the family of the dispossessed house of Moray and espoused its cause. He took a large fleet up the Clyde, supported by men of Ireland and Kintyre, Argyll and the isles; but they were defeated near Renfrew in 1164, Somerled was killed, and his kingdom was passed in fragments to his sons. Chief amongst his descendants are Clan Dougal and Clan Donald. At a time when so many other societies were becoming de-tribalised, that of the Highlands underwent the reverse process, as the erosion of central authority threw people back upon the narrow loyalties of the clan system.

This was when people living on the fringes of the Highlands first saw the curious architecture which symbolised the advent of control by supporters of the Margaretsons in the hostile north. It consisted of a timber strong-

The ruins of Castle Sween with its twelfth-century Norman keep and later additions still stand beside Loch Sween in Knapdale; with Cubbie Roo's (Kolbein Hruga's) Castle in Orkney and the castle of Old Wick in Caithness, it is the earliest surviving stone castle in Scotland.

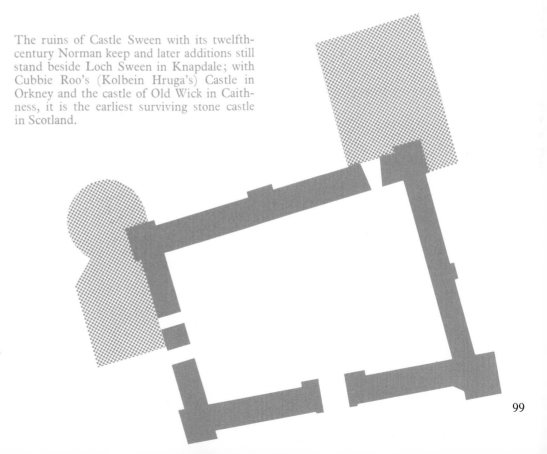

hold erected on an artificial mound, and it was the headquarters of a man who had been granted a feudal tenure over a slice of territory in return for an obligation of military service and the responsibility of controlling the lives of the local inhabitants as loyal subjects of the king. The motte and bailey castle, as it is called, was the embattled outpost of an alien power. The mound of one of them can still be seen at Duffus near Elgin. It marks the defeat of a rebellion in which King Lulach's grandson Angus was killed at Stracathro in 1130. His ancient patrimony of Moray was forfeited to the crown by David I and placed under the feudal rule of one of his supporters, who held the people in submission from this stronghold.

In the course of time the motte and bailey design was replaced by castles of stone. Margaret's eldest son King Edgar had built one of these at Invergowrie before his death in 1107, but the oldest surviving in Scotland belongs to Somerled's kingdom of the west. It stands on a rock overlooking Loch Sween in Knapdale, a stout rectangular enclosure to which a massive square tower was added in the 13th century and a round one later still. On the whole, however, most of the earliest stone castles in Scotland were built in the lands of the Orkney earls in their heyday, and were designed for defence, not a feudal take-over. Castle Sween may or may not belong to the same category: its origins are obscure.

On the little island of Wyre stands the ruins of the little keep now known as Cubbie Roo's. Referring to the 1140s, the Orkney saga relates: 'There lived in Wyre in the Orkneys a Norseman called Kolbein Hruga, and he was the most outstanding of men. He had a fine stone castle built there; it was a safe stronghold.' Bishop Bjarni the poet, who presided over the canonisation of Earl Rognvald, lived in this castle in his youth, for he was Kolbein's son. Its security was tested nearly a century later when an unsuccessful attempt was made to assault it.

There are several other castles of the same period in Orkney, though none so well preserved, and saga references to castles of which no trace remains. On the mainland the castle of Old Wick still stands on its precipitous promontory, while at Dun Creich on the

Sutherland frontier it was probably a Norse tower that stood within the remains of the vitrified fort, overlooking the Dornoch Firth and the province of Moray. Stewart Cruden, the outstanding interpreter of the Scottish castle, has identified Dunyveg in Islay as of Norse origin also.

Meanwhile for another hundred years at least the folk of Jarlshof in Shetland continued to live in peace and prosperity, without any apparent need to look to their defence, and the uneventful record of the community at Freswick in Caithness appears to have been the same. The inhabitants of the Udal in North Uist were less fortunate. The extensions and improvements to their dwellings can be seen to have followed a normal pattern until the time of Magnus Barelegs' destructive raid of 1098. A year or two later a new longhouse was built, on the site amidst the ruins of its predecessors.

What occurred in those inaccessible hinterlands of the northern Highlands, remote from the centres of political strife, remains a mystery. After the descendants of Aodh and his wife had suffered final defeat, what became of the Mackays and their people in Moray? It is possible that through the influence of Aodh's grand-daughter Gormflaith, who was Harold Maddadson of Orkney's wife, they were enabled to settle in the mountainous province west of Caithness once known as Strathnaver, where Norse communities had established themselves in only a few coastal areas such as Tongue and Eriboll. However it occurred, this land became known as Duthaich 'Ic Aoidh, the Country of the Sons of Aodh, and in 1415 the chief of the clan was considered an eligible husband for a sister of the Lord of the Isles. More remarkable still, he was described as the leader of four thousand fighting men, a formidable force by the standard of those days. Perhaps Strathnaver's population was swollen by Moraymen when they were evicted to make room for the settlement of 'loyal' people: perhaps these found to their surprise a sizeable population of people still speaking Pictish in its hidden glens.

In the wake of the new castles, people experienced religious changes that spread

David I, 1124–1153, son of Malcolm III and St Margaret, had lived at the English court, 'his manners thus polished from the rust of Scottish barbarity'(!), continued his mother's Anglo-Norman policy and during his reign founded nine abbeys, an expensive piety which caused James I later to remark that he was 'a sore saint for the crown'.

Malcolm IV, The Maiden, 1153–1165; the nickname arose from the young king's tender years rather than from effeminacy—he was eleven years old when he ascended to the throne on the death of his grandfather, David I, at Carlisle.

Apart from the initial letter of the Charter of Kelso Abbey, 1159, which portrays David I and his grandson Malcolm IV, artists have sought the likeness of the early kings in the great seals of the monarchs with varying invention and skill.

William I, The Lion, 1165–1214, so-called not from his fierce courage but from his interest in law—leo justitiae; William died at the age of seventy-one at Stirling after a long, exhausting if not turbulent, reign.

Alexander III, 1249–1286, succeeded to the throne at the age of seven. In 1266 by the Treaty of Perth he extended his rule to the Isle of Man and the Hebrides; Orkney and Sheland were to remain under Norse domination for a further two hundred years. The last years of his reign are generally celebrated as a Golden Age, a period of peace and prosperity.

David I

Malcolm IV

William I

Alexander III

gradually throughout the region. One of their earliest architects was Turgot from Durham, who became Bishop of St Andrews and wrote the life of St Margaret. In it he spoke of the holy men of the Celtic church, the Céli Dé, or Devotees of God, as 'angels on earth'. Such were the Culdees to whom King Macbeth and Queen Gruoch had made their benefaction. No doubt there were also more worldly members of the old monastic order, especially amongst those who administered valuable properties as founder's kin. Gradually this order was superseded by the organisation of parishes and diocese, planted under the umbrella of the feudal system.

The need for such strong protection was revealed when David I established a bishopric of Caithness which comprehended Sutherland and Strathnaver as well. Andrew the first bishop was recruited from Dunfermline, a daughter house of Canterbury, and it is doubtful whether he was able to reside in his diocese. Certainly the second bishop John was blinded and had his tongue torn out, while the third was roasted over his own fire. Such savage measures reveal how deeply the people of the north resented the harnessing of religion to a policy of subjugation by Anglo-Normans. But by this time these had established a firm base in Sutherland, on the southern edge of the diocese, so here Gilbert was established in greater safety as the fourth bishop, and a cathedral built for him at Dornoch. Very little of it remains in the 19th century church that stands on the spot.

The cathedral of the diocese of Ross was placed likewise in a place surrounded by strong castles and easily reinforced by sea. Its ruins at Fortrose on the Black Isle still display the 13th century undercroft of the chapter house and part of the nave. Of the cathedral of Argyll on the isle of Lismore only the chancel remains, incorporated into the parish church. None of these ever compared in grandeur with St Magnus, Kirkwall, which was being embellished throughout this period.

The parish churches show a similar contrast. Near to Cubbie Roo's castle on Wyre stands the chapel of St Mary, perhaps the earliest of the smaller places of worship, and the most unique is the little round church of Orphir on the Orkney mainland, its shape inspired by the church of the Holy Sepulchre at Jerusalem. It stood unharmed until vandals destroyed most of it in the 18th century to make room for an enlargement of the parish church, and today little more than the apse with its narrow window remains of this memento of St Rognvald's crusade. On the isle of Egilsay, scene of the martyrdom of St Magnus, there still stands a magnificent monument to the country and its people who first brought Christianity to Orkney: a church possessing the round tower of Ireland was built soon after the death of the saint in such a position that it is the most conspicuous landmark in the islands.

In Caithness there are little religious structures at Crosskirk and Lybster that also belong to the 12th century, and in Argyll far to the south, Killean possesses a 12th century nave. As the years passed, parish churches proliferated everywhere, and those of Argyll are especially rich in sculpture, surrounded as they were by the four schools of carving, on the isles of Oronsay and Iona, and in Kintyre and Loch Awe. Some of the chapels, such as the one belonging to the great castle of Dunstaffnage, were much more imposing than the average parish church.

More splendid still were the abbeys and priories of European monastic orders that were introduced into the region. At Beauly north of Inverness there still stands the long narrow nave of one of the only Valliscaulian priories that were ever established outside France—and all are in Scotland. A second was built in 1230 at Ardchattan in Argyll by MacDougal of Lorne, the senior descendant of Somerled, and the third was built at Pluscarden in Moray. In the same year 1230 the abbey of Fearn was founded, and moved eight years later to the fertile promontory of Easter Ross where its ruins may still be seen. Earlier than any of these is the Cistercian monastery of Saddell near Campbelltown, the only religious house in Kintyre, for it was established in the second half of the 12th century, either by Somerled or by one of his sons. On the island of Iona the kindly order of St Benedict superseded that of St Columba.

The apse of the unique round church of Orphir on Orkney mainland. Small, usually rectangular, churches served the communities of the Highlands and Islands for centuries. In contrast splendid monasteries, repositories of learning until the founding of the universities in the fifteenth century were introduced into Scotland under the Canmore kings particularly David I (1124–1153).

These monuments bear witness to the benefits introduced by the regime that was so long and bitterly resisted. Wandering amongst their ruins, and in the precincts of those that have been restored on Iona and at Pluscarden, it is not immediately apparent that they also represent a particular loss.

From the beginning of Christian times it was the churchmen who were the men of letters, and those of the Celtic church had been celebrated for their learning throughout Europe. But they had not only used Latin, the universal language, with Adomnan's elegance. They had also given their own Gaelic language high literary status, preserving in it traditions that dated to pre-Christian times, and refining it as a vehicle for incisive prose and exuberant poetry. After the Gaelic prose of the Book of Deer belonging to about 1100 there are centuries of silence before the next churchman produced the Book of the Dean of Lismore early in the 16th century. For the patrons of the new order belonged to a different cultural tradition.

Outside the Church, distracted Ireland was still capable of fertilising the Gaelic tradition that it had created in Scotland. From Ireland came a member of the bardic family of O'Daly late in the 12th century, named Muireadhach. His descendants were the MacMhuirichs, a name later corrupted to Currie, the longest literary dynasty on record in Europe. At least twenty poems attributed to Muireadhach have survived, one of them addressed to the Earl of Lennox who died in about 1217. Another shows by its contents that it was composed in the Adriatic, and provides supporting evidence that its author took part in the fifth crusade. Another family with a comparable record came from Ireland in the 13th century and became known in Scotland as the Beatons. Their Gaelic medical treatises, derived from the most advanced knowledge of the Greeks, the Arabs and the Salerno school, prove that their scientific contact enabled then to by-pass the medical mumbo-jumbo of much of Christendom in the Middle Ages, while their Gaelic account of the fall of Troy is the earliest to have been translated into any European language out of Greek or Latin.

It took many centuries to reduce a language with such an ancient heritage and such stout supporting pillars to the level of an illiterate peasant speech. To destroy it altogether has proved impossible.

The Norse language was less fortunate, although the auspices for it may have appeared more favourable until several centuries later. But the advent of a succession of Scottish families as earls of Orkney undermined local patronage. The failure of King Haakon IV's expedition in 1263 to reassert his sovereignty over the isles weakened their links with Norway. Gradually the islanders relapsed into provincial isolation.

In 1290 the remarkable dynasty of the Margaretsons expired with the death of a Margaret, the little maid of Norway, sole grand-daughter of Alexander III. The possibility that a King of Norway's daughter might have lived to reign as Queen of Scots is the most alluring might-have-been in the story of the northern isles. As it was, they passed to the Scottish crown after the wars of independence which won it for the dynasties of Bruce and Stewart.

Yet they share fully in the achievement of the peoples of the Highlands and Islands, who have preserved to this day a distinct identity and an indomitable pride in their heritage despite the battering that they were to receive during the next six centuries of history.

St Magnus's church on Egilsay the Orcadian island on which Earl Magnus was murdered in 1117 by Earl Hakon's men. Built after his death the church has a round tower at the west end, a device originating in Ireland in the ninth century when free-standing round towers were built as protection against Viking raids. The walls of the rectangular nave have many small square holes and this has led to the suggestion that the walls were built within wooden shuttering separated by short cross timbers.

Bibliography

The publications listed here are suggested for your further enjoyment. As you will see they form only a small, though very wide-ranging, sample of what is available to you through libraries, museums, societies, official bodies and bookshops. They vary in length from a short article or four page pamphlet to an extensive research published in two volumes and in content from the general to the specialised, from the learned to the popular. All, however, have their particular interest for those who are fascinated by the distant and not so distant past.

Anderson, A. O. & M. O., Eds., **Adomnan's Life of St. Columba,** Nelson, 1961
Barrow, G. W. S., **The Kingdom of the Scots,** Edward Arnold, 1973
Brown, Peter L., **Megaliths, Myths and Men,** Blandford, 1976
Chadwick, Nora K., **Celtic Britain,** Thames & Hudson, 1963
Cole, Sonia, **The Neolithic Revolution,** British Museum (Natural History), 1970
Dickinson, W. Croft, **Scotland from the Earliest Times to 1603,** Oxford Clarendon, 1977
Farrer, James M. P., **Notice of the Runic Inscriptions discovered during recent excavations in the Orkneys,** 1862
Glover, Janet R., **The Story of Scotland,** Faber & Faber, 1977
Hamilton, Ronald, **A Holiday History of Scotland,** Chatto & Windus, 1975
Henderson, Isabel, **The Picts,** Thames & Hudson, 1967
Henshall, Audrey Shore, **The Chambered Tombs of Scotland,** Vols I & II. Edinburgh, 1972
Jones, G., **A History of the Vikings,** Oxford, 1973
Lacaille, D., **The Stone Age in Scotland,** Cambridge, 1964
Menzies, Gordon, Ed., **Who are the Scots?,** BBC London, 1971
Mitchison, Rosalind, **A History of Scotland,** Methuen, 1976
Murray, W. H., **The Islands of Western Scotland,** Eyre Methuen, 1973
Piggott, Stuart, **The Neolithic Cultures of the British Isles,** Cambridge, 1954.
    Ed. **The Prehistoric Peoples of Scotland,** Routledge & Kegan Paul, 1962
    The Druids, Thames & Hudson, 1975
Ponting, Gerald & Margaret, **The Standing Stones of Callanish,** 1977
Renfrew, Colin, Ed., **British Prehistory,** Duckworth, 1974
Ritchie, Anna, **The Kingdom of the Picts,** The Way It Was Series, Chambers, 1977
Rivet, A. L. F., Ed., **The Iron Age in Northern Britain,** Edinburgh, 1966
Roberts, Mark, **Fury of the Vikings,** The Way It Was Series, Chambers, 1977
Ross, A., **Everyday Life of Pagan Celts,** London, 1972
Simpson, W. Douglas, **The Ancient Stones of Scotland,** Robert Hall, 1965
Thom, Alexander, **Megalithic Sites in Britain,** Oxford, 1967
    Megalithic Lunar Observatories, Clarendon Press, 1971

Archaeological Guides
Feachem, Richard, **Guide to Prehistoric Scotland,** Batsford, 1977
MacKie, Euan W., **Scotland: An Archaeological Guide,** Faber & Faber, 1975

Her Majesties Stationery Office publications include:
Jarlshof: J. C. R. Hamilton, 1953
Early Christian and Pictish Monuments: Stewart Cruden, 1964
Scotland, Illustrated Guide to Ancient Monuments: Stuart Piggott & Douglas Simpson, 1970
The Brochs of Mousa and Clickhimin: John Hamilton, 1970
The Neolithic Village at Skara Brae: D. V. Clarke, 1976
Historic Monuments open to the public, List and Map, 1976
Arran: Robert McLelland, 1977

Special Periodicals
Antiquity, A periodic review of archaeology, Ed., Glyn Daniel
Journal for the History of Astronomy, Ed., M. A. Hoskin

The indexes of these and other special periodicals will reveal many articles of particular interest and relevance. For example:
MacKie, Euan W., **Dun Mor Vaul Broch,** etc. Antiquity, Dec. 1965
Renfrew, Colin, **The domestication and exploitation of plants and animals,** Antiquity, Vol 42, 1968
Renfrew, Harkness & Switur, **Quanterness, radiocarbon and the Orkney cairns,** Antiquity, Vol L 199/200, 1976
Thom, A. & A. S., **A Megalithic Lunar Observatory in Orkney: The Ring of Brogar and its cairns,** Journal for the History of Astronomy, Vol 4, 1973
Atkinson, R. J. C., **Megalithic Astronomy—A Prehistorian's Comments,** Journal for the History of Astronomy, 1975.